Abstracts

of

Cumberland County
Virginia
Will Books 1 *and* 2

- 1749-1782 -

By:
Katherine Reynolds

Southern Historical Press, Inc.
Greenville, South Carolina

This volume was reproduced from
A personal copy located in the
Publisher's private library

Please direct all correspondence and orders to:

www.southernhistoricalpress.com
or
SOUTHERN HISTORICAL PRESS, Inc.
PO BOX 1267
Greenville, SC   29601
southernhistoricalpress@gmail.com

Originally published: Easley, SC.   1985
Copyright 1985 by: Southern Historical Press, Inc.
ISBN #0-89308-430-1
All rights Reserved.
Printed in the United States of America

PREFACE

Cumberland County was created in 1749 from the portion of Goochland County south of James River. Its boundaries at that time were Albemarle County (after 1761 Buckingham County) on the west, Amelia County (after 1754 also Prince Edward County) on the south, Chesterfield County on the east and Goochland County on the north. In 1777 the county was divided, its eastern portion forming Powhatan County. In 1778 a small portion of Buckingham County along James River was added to Cumberland County. Since that time there have been no changes in its boundaries.

CUMBERLAND COUNTY, VIRGINIA

Will Book I
1749 - 1792

The first four pages were just fragments.

Page 5: DANIEL JOHNSON, dated October 1746, Pro. February 1749.
          To John Johnson, son of David Johnson and Mary, his wife,
where his father now lives; to John Johnson and Daniel, my work-
ing tool; to John Johnson, son of Daniel and Mary, his wife, all
my wearing apparel; to Elizabeth and Phebe, daughters of Daniel
Johnson and Phebe, his wife, residue of my estate. Ex.: son,
John Johnson. Wit.: Daniel Coleman, Robert Bagby (X), Thos.
Wilks.   Daniel Johnxon (X)

Page 6: Appraisal of estate of DANIEL JOHNSON. March Court 1750.

Page 6: February Court 1740. Non-cupative will of ASHFORD
          HUGHES, deceased, proved by oaths of John Payne, John
McBride, two of the witnesses thereto and on motion of John Woodson, husband of Elizabeth Woodson and legatee of the said will
mentioned and with the consent of Stephen Hughes, heirs at law of
the said Ashford Hughes is admitted to record. Test.: Geo.
Nicholas, C. C. Court.

Inventory of estate of ASHFORD HUGHES, deceased, presented at
November Court 1749.

Page 9: Appraisal of estate of JOHN CREASY in compliance with
          order of February Court 1749. Presented 6 March 1750
by: Wm. Dillon, John Elliott, William Palmer (X).

Page 6: Will of THOMAS HODGES, dated November 1749, Pro. March
          Court 1750. My two sons, William Hodges and John Hodges,
400 acres lying on branches of Willis's creek in Cumberland
county to be equally divided between them; my son, Drury Hodges,
50 acres of land with the plantation whereon he lives; son, Thos.
Hodges, 3 cows and slaves after death of my wife, Christian. Son,
Edm'd. Hodges; daughter, Mary Hodges; son, Thomas Hodges; my
seven children. Ex.: my wife. Wit.: Henry Bell, John Chaffin
(X), William Mills (X).

Page 10: Appraisal of estate of JOSEPH STRANGE. March Court
           1750 by: Thomas Freeman Fretwell, Sam'l. Taylor,
William Dillion.

Page 10: Will of JOHN BUGG, dated 26 April 1750, Pro. June Court
           1750. Son, John Bugg, Benj. Bugg, Sherwood Bugg, all
my children till my youngest child shall then be living may arrive
at age of 18; my wife, Susannah. Ex.: my father, Samuel Bugg
and my brother, Samuel Bugg, Jr. Test.: Ste. Watkins, Richard
Povall, Thos. Hall.   John Bugg (X)

Page 12: Will of JOHN PANKEY, dated 6 October 1749, Pro. June 26,
           1750. Wife, Dorothy, plantation on which I dwell during
her life or widowhood; children, Edward Pankey, John Pankey,
Stephen Pankey, Elizabeth Pankey with unborn babe. Ex.: wife,
Dorothy. Wit.: James Dupuy, Peter Depp (X), Bartholomew Dupuy.
                                    John Pankey (L.S.)

Page 13: Will of PETER GUERRANT of the parish of King William in

1

Cumberland county, dated December 3, 1749, Pro. June 25, 1750. Eldest son, John Guerrant, land on Joshua Creek, one of the branches of the River in Albermarle county; son, Peter Guerrant, land on Hunt's Creek on branch of State River in Albermarle county; son, Daniel Guerrant, land joining land of John; daughter Esther, land when she shall attain age of 21; daughter, Magdalene Guerrant, land on Mountain's Creek in Amelia county, part of the 400 a., after she attain age of 21 or married; daughter, Jane, land; daughter, Judith Guerrant; my wife, Magdalene Guerrant, should she be with child and should it be a boy, I give him 365 lbs. and if a daughter, 16 lbs. after death of my wife plantation to be sold and money divided between my children. Ex.: wife, Magdalene. Wit.: William Salley, Peter Guerrant, David and Richard....(blurred).

Page 13: Will of ROBERT WALTON, dated February 1746(?), Pro. 26 June 1750. Son, John, land on James River; son, Robert, 400 a. in Albermarle county; wife, Mary if she be with child, the negro willed to son, Robert, be equally divided with the child and son, Robert when the youngest comes of age. Ex.: my wife, Mary Walton. Wit.: Anthony Hughes, Samuel Carter, Eliz. Hughes (X).   R. Walton (L.S.)

Codicil proved by oath of witnesses thereto 23 May 1757 in Cumberland county.

Page 17: Codicil: to my son, John and his heirs, 150 a. land where I now live; son, Robert and his heirs, 600 or 700 a. land on Stanton River; to my daughter, Sarah and the child my wife now goes with; to son, Robert, 125 a. in Cumberland county. Ex.: Tucker Woodson, George Walton. Wit.: Sherwood Walton, ...   Robert Walton (L.S.)

Page 18: Appraisal of Estate of THOMAS LOW, deceased. 27 March 1750. By: Jacob Mosby, William Moss, James Moss.

Page 18: Appraisal of Estate of ANTHONY LAVILLIAN, deceased. February 17, 1750. By: John Chastain, James Harris, Isaac Duloy.

Page 19: Inventory of estate of JOHN PANKEY, and appraisal by: Stephen Mallet, Daniel Gorre(?), Thos. Wooldrege.

Appraisal of estate of VINCENT LACY, deceased. 23 July 1750. By: Thos. Carter, George Wright, John Ritchason (X).

Page 21: Inventory of estate of ROBERT WALTON, 23 July 1750. By: Sam Jame(?), Daniel Coleman, Robert Bagby (X).

Page 22: Inventory of estate of JOHN BUGG, 23 July 1750. By: Thomas Halles, Henry Clay, Jr., Thos. Lockett.

Page 23: Appraisal of estate of RICHARD DUDLEY, deceased. June 1750.

Appraisal of estate of THOS. HODGE, 21 April 1750. By: Daniel Coleman, Sr., Joseph Terry, Daniel Coleman, Jr.

Page 24: Appraisal of estate of PETER GUERRANT, deceased, September Court 1750. By: Peter David, Benj. Harris, James Harris.

August 1750. I received of Magdalene Guerrant exr. of Peter
Guerrant, deceased, sum of 20 pounds 7 sh. and 6 pence current
money in full satisfaction of and for my demand by right of my
wife from the estate of Daniel Guerrant, deceased, and also my
wife's right to the estate of her two deceased children, Daniel
and Peter Guerrant, the account relating thereto being this day
settled and Arbitrated by Thomas Turpin, John Harris and George
Carrington. Jos. Bingley, Jacob Trabue. Rec'd. from Samuel
Weaver.

September Court 1750. Cumberland Court This receipt from Samuel
Weaver on the motion of the said Magdalene Guerrant ordered
recorded.

Page 27: August 10, 1750. Received of Magdalene Guerrant ex. of
        Peter Guerrant, deceased, sum of 30 pounds 10 sh. 11
pence in full satisfaction of my demand against the estate of
Daniel Guerrant, deceased by right of my wife and also full of
my right and demand for my wife's part of the estate of my wife's
deceased brothers, Daniel and Peter Guerrant....Rec'd. Charles
Perro(?).

Page 27: 8 February 1743. I, Jacob Trabue of the Parish of King
        William in the County of Henrico have bargained and
sold unto Peter Guerrant of the aforesaid parish in Goochland
county, one negro girl named Sarey and do warrant the said Negro
girl Sarey from all person or persons or claim. Test.: John
Trabue, Clark Trabue (X), Ede Lark(?)(X).

This Bill of Sale from Jacob Trabue to Peter Guerrant recorded
September Court 1750.

Page 28: Will of ANN DAVID, of the Parish of King William in
        Cumberland county, dated 10 October 1750, Pro. November
1750. To Mary Ann Burton, my wearing clothes; to Lewis Burton,
10 pounds for schooling my daughter Ann Easley; remainder of my
estate to be sold and divided between my three children, Peter
David, Ann Easley and Mary Ann Burton. Ex.: son, Peter David.
Wit.: Samuel Weaver, Peter Faure (X), David LeSueur.

Page 29: Will of NORVILL BASKERVILLE, dated 9 May 1750, Pro.
        February Court 1751. To my brother, George, all my
real and personal estate. Ex.: brother, George Baskerville.
Wit.: Henry Norvell, John Cardwell, Richard Cardwell

January Court 1750. Appointed to appraise estate of ELIZABETH
BARNARD, deceased. Recorded by Job Thomas, Benjamin Harrison,
Thomas Tabb, Alexander Trent. Manniken Town, February Court 1750.

Page 31: Will of JAMES MEREDITH, dated February 27, 1750, Pro.
        March Court 1751. Wife, Martha Meredith, land I lately
bought of Mary Webb, situate on both sides of the branches of
Deep Creek during her widowhood, then to daughter, Christina,
land I bought of Stephen Hughes and Booth Hopper and also land I
now live on to be sold by my exrs. if necessary to pay my debts.
My friends, John Fleming and William Meggison to collect the
several outstanding debts now owing me; my friend, Benjamin
Harris, finish my business in the several courts. Ex.: wife,
Martha Meredith, Capt. Francis James, John Fleming, Jr., and
William Megginson and guardians of daughter, Christina appoint,
Capt. Francis James, Major Archibald Cary, Benjamin Harris of
Manniken Town. Wit.: Robt. Goldie, Jos. Apperson, Ben. Harris.

Will of ISAAC GOODWIN of county of Goochland and King
William Parish, dated 11 August 1745, Pro. March Court
1751. Wife, Ann Goodwin; my two Granddaughters, Judith Fore,
Judith Agee. Wit.: John Ford, Simon Droman, John Pompham,
Matthew Agee (X).   Isaac Goodwin (X)

Page 34: Will of ABRAHAM ALLEN of Cumberland county, dated
          20 May 1750, Pro. May Court 1751. Wife, Mary and child
she goes with, land joining John Allen and Thomas Smith. Ex.:
wife, Mary. Wit.: Anthony Morgan, Agnes Morgan, John Winfree,
Mary Walton.   Abraham Allen (X)

Page 35: Will of JOSEPH HOOPER, dated 25 December 1750, Pro.
          May Court 1751. Wife, Elizabeth; to Elizabeth Stinson;
son-in-law, Henry Trent, 200 a. land whereon he now lives; to
John Stinson, my silver watch; nephew, Hugh Hooper; Joseph Stinson; to my nephew, George Hooper, my Bible. Care of this will
to my friend, George Carr. Ex.: wife, Elizabeth Hooper. Wit.:
William Howard, John Stinton(?).

Page 37: Will of JOHN HARRIS of King William Parish in Cumber-
          land county, dated 23 March 1751, Rec. May Court 1751.
To Brother Benjamin Harris, 54 acres; to brother William Harris,
land I purchased of Susanna Carnes; to James Mobley, land lying
on North side of Fluvanna River in Albermarle county; to my
daughter, Elizabeth Flournoy; granddaughter, Ursley Flournoy;
son, John Harris, land on Jones' Creek adjoining Robert Good and
Capt. Thomas Carter; three brothers, James, Benjamin and John
Harris, if son John Harris should desire and choose his guardian
that neither he nor his guardian shall have any possession until
my said son arrives to 21 years; my sister, Sarah Harris, shall
live in my house until my son John arrives to 21 years. Ex.:
three brothers, James Harris, Benjamin Harris, William Harris
and Samuel Flournoy. Wit.: Bennett Goode, Charles Clark.

Page 39: May Court 1751. Account of Sale of ANN DAVID, late of
          King William Parish, deceased. Names listed: John
Godsey, Richard Pemberton, Robert Hudson, John James Dupuy,
Joseph Bingley, Thomas Robertson, Peter David, Thomas Ellison,
Henry Hatcher, James Meredith, David Thomas, Mary Ann Burton,
Robert Woolridge, Jacob Trabue, John Hall, Joseph Sharpe, Matthew
Bingley, Wm. Soblet, Peter David, Robert Hudson, David LeSueur,
John Young, Mary Goog, Charles Perro, John Butler, Abraham Salley,
Edward _____, William Harrison, William Spiers, William Patteson,
Thomas Godsey, Peter Baillend, Henry Winfrey, John Larlain, Perrin
Giles, Thomas Lacy.

Page 42: By order of the Court: Appraisal of land improvements
          of land of JOSEPH BUTLER lying on....and bounded by
John Holloway, Paul Michaux, Job Thomas, and James Anderson.
May 27, 1751

Page 42: Will of JAMES BARNES, no date, Rec. 22 July 1751. Son,
          John, my tract of land at Nottoway, when of age; if
wife is with child, my land on....; son, James, land where on
Selcock lives, Blemstone; son, Francis; son, George, land whereon
I live after death of mother; daughter, Sarah Barnes; daughter,
Mary; daughter, Martha. Will presented by widow, Mary and sworn
as witnesses: Nicholas Hoyle and Nicholas Hoyle, Jr. Sec.
Bartholomew Stovall and William Smith.

Page 44: ALEXANDER TRENT, dated 9 December 1750, Pro. July 22,
          1751, of Southam Parish. To son, Peterfield Trent,

4

400 a. of land, part in Cumberland and part in Albermarle; 700 a. whereon Thomas Johns now lives to son, Alexander Trent; all rest of my lands to Daughter, Elizabeth Trent to her at age 16; wife, Frances Trent; also my desire that Robert Johns have sufficient corn found him at Field's plantation Brookses Hill they can provided or make corn for the plantation. Wit.: James Terry, William Trigg, Samuel Allen.

Page 47:   Appraisal of estate of THOMAS CARDWELL, July Court 1751.
           By: John Woodson, Benjamin Childrey, Samburn Woodson,
Peter LeGrand.

Page 48:   Inventory and Sale of estate of WILLIAM BURTON, deceased.
           December 11, 1749.

Page 49:   Inventory of estate of JAMES BARNES, JR., 14 May 1751.

Page 51:   Account of the Estate of FRANCIS JAMES, JR. Returned
           August 27, 1750, March 1751; September 12, 1750,
June 26, 1751; October 20, 1750, August 3rd, 1751.

Page 51:   Will of ISAAC DULAY, of King William Parish in county
           of Cumberland, but now in Lunenburg, dated 26 November
1750, Pro. March Court 1752. Nephew Duloy Porter, son of Thomas
Porter, 400 a. in Cumberland county which land was heretofore
granted by letters patent to Peter Duloy to be delivered when he
come of age; to Elizabeth Branch, daughter of Thomas Porter; my
sister, Mary Ann Goss, one piece of land left to me in John
Peter Bilboe's last will lying in Cumberland county; to Thomas
Porter and his wife....Ex.: Thomas Porter. Wit.: James Bilbo,
John James, John Maxey.   Signed: Isaac Duloy L.S.

Page 52:   Will of JOHN CANNIFAX, dated February 7, 1752, Pro.
           March Court 1752. Son, John Cannifax, all my land
lying between the main road of Jones' Creek; son, James Cannifax,
in lieu of a joynture(?) made to the said James' mother of 100
pounds to be settled on the heir of my body begotten on her, all
my land and plantation lying between the main road and fine(?)
creek, also my part of "Fine" creek mill to be held by him after
death of said mother to whom I give the use during her life then
to said James; my daughter, Mary, 30 pounds; my daughter, Elizabeth, 5 pounds; I give to be equally divided amongst my beloved
wife, John, Edward and William Cannifax. Ex.: my wife and John
Cannifax. Wit.: Thomas Turpin, Joseph Akin, John Epperson.

Page 54:   Appraisal of estate of Capt. JAMES BARNES, deceased.
           22 January 1752.

           Inventory of estate of Capt. JAMES BARNES, deceased,
           returned March Court 1752.

           Will of WILLIAM MONROW(?) of Goochland county, Novem-
           ber 28, 1743, Pro. May Court 1752. To my eldest son,
Francis; my two youngest sons; rest of my children as follows:
Elizabeth, William, Samuel, James, Benjamin, Edward, Dancy and
Stephen. Exrs.: Son, Francis and William. Wit.: Joseph
Fuquay (X), William Fuquay, Jr. (X).
                              William Monrow(?) (X)

Page 56:   Will of WILLIAM WALKER of Southam Parish in Cumberland
           county, dated 22 May 1752, Pro. May Court 1752. Son,
James, 350 a. and plantation where James Spradlin now lives
running from back line of Edward Davidson to Appomattox River;

5

Son, Warren Walker, 400 a. together with plantation where I now
live, with plantation where John Duram now lives; my five sons,
Joel, Peter, Robert, Benjamin and Henry, 80 pounds; to my two
daughters, Lucy and Judy, 3 pounds; if any of my 5 sons die before
they reach age of 20 and the same of my two daughters, my will is
that my wife, Judy Walker should have a good maintenance out of
the estate; my son, Warren Walker to have full care of negroes
and personal estate to fullfill this my last will and testament.
Ex.: my wife, Judy Walker and son, Warren Walker. Wit.: David
Davison, Stephen Wood, James Reynold (X).

William Walker

Page 52: Will of HENRY MARTAIN, dated January 25, 1750, Pro. May
Court 1752. Wife, Susanner(?) Martain; my four sons:
William, Henry, John and Benjamin Martain; Amie Martain, Drusilla;
Ann Martain. Ex.: my wife Susanner Martain, William Arnold.
Wit.: John Bostick, Thomas Duling.

Page 55: Inventory of estate of ISAAC DULOY, 26 March 1752.

Page 59: Will of PETER (PIERRE) SALLEE of King William Parish
in Cumberland county, 24 December 1750, Pro. 27 November 1752. Wife, Frances; sons, Isaac and Abraham, 400 a. land in
Albermarle county, lying on Troublesome Creek; daughter, Mary;
daughter, Judith; son, Jacob; ....land I now live on. Ex.: wife,
Frances and John Bondurant. Wit.: Thomas Turpin, Jo. Bondurant,
Thomas Bradley. Signed Pierre Salle

Page 60: Will of RICHARD FAIN, dated 29 January 1752, Pro. 20
February 1753. Wife, Sarah Fain; sons, Joel Fain,
Daniel Fain, John Fain; granddaughter, Kezie Fain; daughters,
Elizabeth Epperson, Mary Easlock, Sarah Edwards. Ex.: wife,
Sarah and two sons, Daniel and Joel. Wit.: Geo. Carrington,
Ronert Douglas.

Page 60: Will of STEPHEN HUGHES of Cumberland County, dated
6 July 1749, Pro. 26 January 1752. ....shall sell land
on Randolph's Creek by estimation 1600 a. to pay my debts and
money left to be divided between my daughter, Judith Cox and my
son, John; and whereas there shall be some land unsold in hands
of Col. Mayo's exrs. my will is that when sold money be paid my
son, John; also son, John to have land I now live on; my wife,
Elizabeth, three slaves during her life; said slaves to go to
Joseph Hughes at my wife's death; my daughter, Elizabeth Woodson.
Exrs.: my wife, Elizabeth and son, Joseph Hughes. Wit.: John
Robinson, Robert Hughes, Judith Bergamy.

Page 65: Appraisal of estate of JOHN DOBIE, deceased. 23 July
1753. William Trigg, Daniel Coleman, William Daniels

Page 62: Appraisal of estate of PETER SALLEY, deceased. December 6, 1752. By: William Maxey, Thomas Bradley,
Daniel or David Penons(?).

Page 63: Sale of estate of PETER SALLEY, December 25, 1752.

Page 64: Appraisal of slaves and personal estate of STEPHEN
HUGHES, 21 July 1753.

Page 66: Appraisal of estate of JOHN GILLS, 23 March 1752. By:
William Diller, William Palmer.

Page 67: Sale of estate of JOHN GILLS, 22 June 1752. Buyers:

Andrew Edwards, John Mackenny, Thomas Carter, John
Elliott, Michel Rowland, William Dullion, Littleberry Mosbey,
William Swann, Robert Carter, Elizabeth Carroll, Sam'l. Taylor,
Thomas Redford, Micajah Mosby, Charles Mackenny, William Trigg.

Page 68: Inventory of estate of WILLIAM WALKER, July 8, 1752.
          By: Judy Walker (X), Warren Walker, Henry Moss(?).

Page 68: Inventory of JOHN HARRIS, deceased, November 27, 1751.
          By: Thomas Smith, James Robinson, Jr., Bennet Goode.

Page 70: Will of JOHN FORD of Cumberland County and King William
          Parish, 3 September 1753, Pro. 24 September 1753. My
beloved brother, JAMES FORD: sister, Mary Fuqua; sister, Judith
Leake; to Peter Bondurant, my household goods, etc. Ex.: John
Leake and William Fuqua, if my brother Daniel dies without heirs,
it falls to Peter Ford. Wit.: Isaac Sallee, James Smith, Allen
Criddle.

Page 72: Will of SARAH HARRIS of Cumberland County, dated 12
          April 1753, Pro. 24 September 1753. To brother, James
Harris; to brother, Benjamin Harris; to brother, William Harris;
nephew, John Harris, Sr.; sister, Mary James; sister, Eadith
Patrick; sister, Ann Booth; niece, Elizabeth Flournoy; three
brothers, James Harris, Benjamin Harris, William Harris. Ex.:
James Harris, Benjamin Harris and William Harris. Wit.: James
Holman, James Smith.

Page 73: Will of JOHN RICHARDSON, 22 June 1753, Pro. September
          24, 1753. Son, Isham Richardson, plantation whereon I
now live and 500 a. of land, land I own on Hodnett's Creek in
Albermarle county, except 66 a. on South side of Hodnett's Creek
being little Willises which belongs to John Hannaway, Jr. and it
is my desire that my son, John may have 2 a. of said land on
South side of said creek which is intended to build a mill and
that he and his brother, Isham may be partners in said mill which
I give to him; my son, John, 800 a. on Cub Creek in Lunenburg
County; daughter, Elizabeth Richardson, 320 a. on Lickinghole
Creek in Goochland County; daughter, Mary Richardson, 300 a.
joining land I now live on; daughter, Martha Richardson, 200 a.
on Mill Creek; daughter, Ann Richardson, 200 a. on Buffalow River
in Amelia county; daughter, Sarah Richardson, 200 a.; daughter,
Susannah Richardson, 200 a.; daughter Agnes Richardson, 200 a.;
daughter, Frances Richardson, remaining part of said tract; wife,
Mary Richardson. Exrs.: friends, John Gannaway, Obediah Woodson, Charles Anderson. Wit.: Roger Williams, William Brown (X).
                                              John Richardson (X)

Page 76: Appraisal of slaves and personal estate of STEPHEN
          HUGHES, 24 September, 1753. By: Daniel Coleman, Robert
Bagby, Francis James.

          Estate of ANTHONY LAVILLION, deceased, to Elizabeth
          Lavillion, administratrix, November 20, 1753.

Page 81: Will of WILLIAM HARRISON, late of Chesterfield County,
          dated 7 August 1753, Pro. 24 September 1753. To my
mother, Sarah Harrison, plantation whereon I now live; wife,
Elizabeth; to the person or persons now claiming piece of land
in King William County under the title of my half brother,
Ezekiel Slaughter, who formerly sold the said land to John Drury
and I claiming a right thereto having consideration thereof been
paid and contented by the said half brother, do release to the

said person claiming by the above said title, money in my Uncle Samuel....hands; my daughter, Molley Harrison; son, William. Ex.: half brother, Ezekiel Slaughter, brother-in-law, Israel Winfree. Wit.: George Benn(?) Turner, John Harrison (X), Mary Jenning.

Page 93: Inventory of estate of SARAH HARRIS, October 19, 1753. By: James Harris, Benjamin Harris, William Harris.

Page 93: Appraisal of estate of THOMAS MARTAIN, June 11, 1754. By: Stephen Bedford, John Baskerville, John Nailey.

Page 94: Will of WILLIAM MOSS of Cumberland County, dated 30 September 1753, Pro. 23 September 1754. Wife, Elizabeth; son, Thomas Moss, land and plantation lying and being in New Kent County; grandson, James Moss, land I bought of John Rixby; grandson, John Moss; son, William Moss; daughter, Tabitha Stoval; son, James Moss; daughter, Ann Allyn. Ex.: sons, Thomas and William and James. Wit.: Edward Tabb, Thomas Payton, Elizabeth Bandy (X).

Page 96: Will of MATHIAS CHEATWOOD of Southam Parish in Cumberland County, 28 June 1752; 27 June 1754(?). Son, Andrew Cheatwood; son, Richard; wife, Mary; son, Mathias, 100 a. on Turkey Creek Branch, also 100 a. adjoining Joseph Baugh's upper line and Abraham Baugh's land; son, John Cheatwood; son, James Cheatwood. Ex.: wife and son, Richard. Wit.: Daniel Fore, Isham Akin, Abraham Baugh.

Page 97: Will of JOHN MORSSUM (MORSHAM?), dated 7 October 1754, 27 January 1755. Wife, Elizabeth, 400 a. land part of 600 a. in Albermarle County; to Mary Blackburn, daughter of William Blackburn, deceased, 200 a. of land in Albermarle County. Ex.: wife, Elizabeth and John Blackburn. Wit.: Richard Ligon, Blackburn Akers(?), Thomas Baley.

Will of PETER LOUIS SOBLETT of King William Parish in Cumberland County, 5 November 1754, 27 January 1755. Sons, Peter, William and Abraham Soblett; son, Lewis Soblett, land in Chesterfield County; son, Benjamin Soblett. Ex.: William Soblett and Lewis Soblett. Wit.: Jos. Bingley, Ginkins Self (X), Abraham Self(?). Joseph Bingley and William Soblett made bond.

Page 90: Will of JEREMIAH COX of Southam Parish in Cumberland County, dated 4 May 1754, Pro. 27 January 1755. Son, William Cox, gun that was my grandfather's; son, Edward, land on upper side of Mohooch Creek; son, William Cox; wife, Elizabeth, to have plantation; son, John Cox; my five daughters, Mary, Elizabeth, Phebe, Jane and Fanny and my son, John to go to school space of three whole years. Ex.: wife and son, William Cox. Wit.: Anthony Morgan, Harry Bagby, Susannah Bagby, John Epperson, William Walker, Isaac Hughes.

Appraisal of estate of DANIEL SCOTT, deceased, 20 January 1755. By: Thos. Porter, Benjamin Harris, James Holman.

Page 94: Inventory of estate of DANIEL SCOTT returned and ordered recorded, May 26, 1755.

Page 95: Inventory and appraisal of SAMUEL SCOTT, 23 June. John Merryman, Thomas Walker, Joco(?) Sinfree.

Page 96:   Estate of WILLIAM REYNOLDS, deceased. 23 June 1755.
           By: John Bailey, Daniel Williams, Joseph Johns (X).

           Will of JOHN JOHNSON of Parish of Southam in Cumberland
           County, 4 February, 1755; 23 June 1755. Wife, Sarah;
son, Joseph Johnson; daughter, Martha Johnson; appoint John Winfrey and Joseph Johnson guardians of my two children and likewise
of my whole estate. Wit.: Francis James, William Pledge, Jacob
Michaux.   John Johnson (X)

           Inventory of estate of FREDERICK COX and appraisal,
           3 May 1755. By: Francis James, Robert Bagby (X), Jos.
Hughes.

Page 100: Will of JOELL CHANDLER, last day February 1754, Pro.
           20 July 1755. Wife, Prisilah Chandler, one half of
land during his life; son, Robert, son of Joel Chandler and
Prisilah Chandler his wife, my dwelling place and one half of
land; son, David Chandler, son of Joel and Prisciler, his wife,
the other half of tract of land I now live on; son, John Chandler;
son, Jesse Chandler; son, Timothy Chandler; daughter, Rebecca
Chandler. Ex.: wife, Prisilah Chandler and son, Robert Chandler.
Wit.: Edward Dovall, John Crugg (X), Edwin Tonny, Charley Tonney
(X).

Page 102: Appraisal of JOHN JOHNSON. Philip Webber, Jr., Joseph
           Woodson, Henry Turner.

           Appraisal of estate of THOS. FLIPPEN, 23 August 1755.
           John Merryman, Jacob Winfree, Thomas Walker.

Page 103: Appraisal of MATTHEW CHEATWOOD, August 22, 1755. By:
           Henry Clay, Joseph Baugh, Abraham Baugh.

Page 104: Appraisal of estate of JOHN MOSOMS, 25 August 1755.
           Henry Clay, John Moseley, Nathaniel Maxey.

Page 105: Will of ROBERT HUGHES, 13 July 1750, Pro. 22 September
           1755. Wife, Martha Hughes; eldest daughter, Sarah
Woodson; 2nd daughter, Mary Woodson; 3rd daughter, Martha Walton;
4th daughter, Susanna Hughes; brother, Ashfords; 5th daughter,
Temperance Hughes; son, Abraham Hughes; leave land and plantation
I hold on each side of Muddy Creek to use of my wife, Martha,
during her natural life or widowhood; oldest son, Robert. Ex.:
wife. Wit.: John Robinson, Judith Bergamy. Codicil: 25 October 1752. Daughter, Susanna Hughes, 80 pounds and a negro woman;
daughter, Temperance Hughes, 50 pounds. Wit.: John Epperson,
Judith Bergamy.

Page 107: Inventory of estate of JOEL CHANDLER, 12 August 1755.
           By: John Franklin, Robert Bagby, Bob Stovall.

Page 198: Inventory of estate of WILLIAM HARRISON, September 22,
           1755.

Page 109: Appraisal of estate of THOS. FLIPPEN, 24 November 1755.
           Thomas Walker, Ralph Flippen, John Merryman.
                              Pd. John Roland

Page 110: Pd. Murry; Pd. Macky; Moses Smith. One wescoat for
           Wm. Flippen; one pair shoes for Wm. Flippen; three
pair shoes of Holland(?) for Elizabeth Flippen; 9 yards of
Swankin(?) for Anne Flippen; one pair shoes for Ann Flippen;

coat for Anne Flippen; two yards Holland for Thos. Flippen; 1 pair
shoes for Thos. Flippen; three....for Thomas Flippen. Signed:
Thomas Walton, Ralph Flippen, John Merryman.

Page 110: Appraisal of estate of JOHN HOLLOWAY, deceased. Sworn
           to before Stephen Bedford gentlemen one of his Majes-
tie's Justices, 24 November 1755. By: John Merryman, Wm. Bond,
Richard Murry.

Page 111: MARGARET RANINE of Parish of King William, dated
           8 March 1755, Pro. 26 January 1756. Grandson, Anthony
Martin; grandson, John Martin; grandson, Peter Martin; of my
daughter Mary Ann; my husband, Anthony Raneee(?); if any money
should fall to me from any of my relatives from Holland or France
or England or any other parts for my son, Daniel Perron and Mary
Fany two parts the other two parts for the children of my daughters deceased Ann and Mary Ann. Ex.: Daniel Perron and James
Holman. Wit.: Daniel Perron, Peter Bondurant, Stephen Perron.
Pro. 26 January 1756   Margaret Ranine(?) (X)

Page 112: WILLIAM PARKER of Parish of Southam, dated 24 August
           1755, Pro. 22 March 1755. Wife, Drusilla Parker;
daughter, Elizabeth, two negroes Diner, daughter of Sarah and
Diblin, son of Sarah; my three sons, Daniel, Obediah and William,
land I obtained by deed of my father; to son, Daniel, land in
Halifax county. Ex.: my father, Richard Parker, my brother,
Richard Parker. Wit.: Anthony Colquit, Richd. Daniel, Laurence
Smith, Anthony Christian.

Page 116: LAMBOURN WOODSON(?) of Southam Parish, dated 13 Nov-
           ember 1755, Pro. 28 June 1756. Wife, Charity Woodson;
son, Hughes; my five children, Hughes Woodson,...., Jane Woodson,
Jesse Woodson, Mary Ann Woodson. Ex.: wife, Charity. Wit.:
Ann Owen, William Tabor, Susannah Ferris (X).
The name "Woodson" was not clear. Lambourn Woodson

Page 114: GEORGE WILLIAMSON, dated 18 January 1756, Pro. 28 June
           1756. Son, George, the river part of the tract of
land I now live on beginning at a corner Buller(?) wood standing
in....Creek along line to Old Road thence down said road to Back
line....; my son, Robert Williamson, all the residue and remainder of said tract; my wife and children; after debts are paid the
residue to son George till he come of age 18, then to be equally
divided between all my children. Ex.: son, George Williamson,
Arthur Masally(?), Edward Bass. Wit.: Chas. Ballew, Wm. Marshall,
Edw'd. Mosley(?), Thos. T. Hamley (X).
                              George W. Williamson (X)

           JOSEPH HUGHES of Southam Parish, dated 25 November
           1755, Pro. 29 June 1756. To Henry Hobson and his
heirs, 200 a. and being part of tract I now live on and them 200
a. provided by pay my exors. 55 pounds; my brother, John Hughes,
225 a. being land given him by my father; my loving wife, 250 a.
land which was given me by my father; to my loving wife, Jane,
7 negroes; to my loving wife, all my personal estate except my
saddle and bridle which I give to my brother John; to my Mother
Elizabeth Hughes, slaves during her life then to my brother,
John Hughes. Ex.: wife, Jane Hughes, John Hughes, William Hobson. Wit.: Richard James, Thomas Poindexter, Ann Atkinson.

This last will and testament of Joseph Hughs was presented by
Thomas Poindexter and Ann Atkinson two of the witnesses and order
to be recorded and Jane Hughes executrix. John Hughes, Jr. and

William Hobson exors. therein named refused to serve and upon
motion of John Woodson, guardian to John Hughes heir of the said
deceased who made oath according to law was granted letter of
administration.

Pursuant to order of court 22 June 1756, appointed to appraise
estate of WILLIAM PARKER, Robt. Thomson, George Cox and Henry
Cox; returned appraisal.

July 17, 1756: Inventory of estate of GEORGE WILLIAMSON. By:
Arthur Moseley, Edward Bass. Inventory was ordered recorded
17 September 1756.

Page 119: DAVID THOMAS of St. James Parish of Cumberland County.
          Dated 16 July 1756, Pro. 27 September 1756. Unto
William Howard of King William Parish, 39 pounds to be paid him
after death of me and my wife, Elizabeth; unto Rebecca Lochado(?),
daughter (under 18) of....of King William Parish after death of
me and my wife; Judith   Lochado, youngest sister of Rebecca....;
to Elizabeth Lookadoo, wife of Peter Lookadoo(?). Ex.: Peter
Lookado(?), William Howard. Wit.: David Leseuer, Samuel Weaver,
Peter David.

          Inventory of estate of WILLIAM MOSS, JR., deceased,
          pursuant to order 23 August 1756 was returned and
recorded. September 20, 1756 by Jacob Moseley, Jas. Mosley, Benj.
Mosley.

Page 122: JOHN FLEMING, dated 29 May 1756, Pro. 27 December 1756.
          Son, John; son, Charles, land on Willises Creek; son,
Thomas Fleming, land on James River in Goochland County called
Little Creek tract; son, William Fleming, tract called Mount
Pleasant being land whereon I now live; son, Richard, stand in
Goochland County called Dover tract or plantation; daughter, Mary
Bernard; daughter, Caroline Fleming; division of personal estate
to be made by friends George Carrington, Archibald Cary and Wade
Metherland. Ex.: son, John, Thomas and William. Wit.: Richard
Furlong, Tarlton Fleming, Bathcroft Shelton.
                                        John Fleming

Page 125: Appraisal of estate of CARENLIUS C...., returned 24
          September 1756.

Page 125: JOHN SMITH of King William Parish, date 29 May 1755,
          Pro. 20 February 1757. My wife, Jane; son, Abraham
Smith; son, Childarson Smith; son, James Clarksander Smith; son,
Joseph Smith; son, John; daughter, Mary Blankenship. Ex.: wife,
Jane, son, John Smith. Wit.: Thos. Hall, William Maxey (X),
Nathaniel Maxey.

Page 127: RICHARD EPPERSON, dated March 3, 1757, Pro. March 12,
          1758. Son, Richard, parcel of land on S side of
Joneses' Creek; son, Frances Radford Epperson, 150 a. on the
same branch, part of the same tract; son, John Epperson, 150 a.
remainder of same tract; daughter, Agnes, one feather bed,
furniture, etc.; rest of estate to my wife, Susanna. Ex.:
Susanna Epperson and Frances Epperson and John Radford Epperson.
Wit.: John Epperson, Thos. Epperson, Sarah Bondurant (X).
                                        Richard Epperson L.S.

Page 128: Appraisal of estate of BENJAMIN MOSELEY, 28 March 1757.
          Returned by: Henry Clay, John Watkins, Edward Watkins.

11

Page 129: Appraisal of estate of WILLIAM BOLLING. Ordered rec.: September 12, 1756. Made by: Henry Dillon, William Palmer (X), William Dillen.

Page 130: Inventory and appraisal of estate of SANBORN WOODSON, order recorded 23 May 1757. By: Benjamin Childrey, Francis Marcran, Jos. Woodson.

Page 131: Inventory of JOSEPH STRANGE, order recorded April 3, 1757. By: Wm. Sledge(?), Benj.....(too pale to read), William....(too pale to read).

Account of sale of Estate of JOSEPH STRONG presented to Thomas Pleasant his administrator. Ordered Rec. 27 May 1757.

Page 132: Inventory of LE VILLAIN, deceased, 24 August 1754. Ordered recorded August 26, 1754 by: John Chastain, James Harris, James Holman.

Page 133: Division of ANTHONY LE VILLAIN. Due orphan of Anthony Le Villain 2/3 of personal estate according to the law; Balance due orphans of slaves; Balance due of profits for 3 years; Balance due orphan 2/3 of amount of the crop made in year 1753. John Chastain, James Harris, James Holman.

Settlement of account of Joseph Le Villain with his wife and orphan and the said Joseph Starkey and his wife for nursing and clothing the orphan for 5 years ending 20 March 1755; Sundry expenses; Nursing one negro child 3 years; nursing one negro child one year and a half. John Chastain, James Harris, James Holman. Rec. 25 August 1755.

Page 134: Appraisal of estate of DAVID THOMAS, 27 September 1756; Rec. 23 May 1757. By: James Harris, Thos. Parker, Chas. Clark.

Page 136: Will of MICHAEL ROWLAND, date 30 March 1757, Pro. 23 May 1757. Wife, Ann Rowland, all my stock and household goods; my crop of tobacco to be sold and that Benjamin Cannon who I appoint executor pay himself 13 pounds 13 sh. which is the balance due him for 100 a. of land I bought of him and where I now live and then the sd. Cannon to acknowledge deed to my son, William Rowland. Wit.: Jeremiah Cannon, Stephen Carter (X), Sam'l. Taylor.   Michael Rowland (X)

Page 137: Inventory of Estate of ROBERT HUGHES, deceased. Dated 1 November 1755, Rec. 28 June 1757. Extrx.: Martha Hughes.

Page 138: EDWARD YARBROUGH, dated March 4, 1749/50, Pro. 22 August 1757. Wife, Elizabeth, sole executrix; daughter, Hannah Yarbrough, land and plantation whereon I now live containing 100 acres; estate after her mother's decease. Wit.: John Maulden, James Hancock, Benjamin Raden.
                Ed. Yarbrough L.S.

Page 139: Appraisal of estate of MICHAEL ROWLAND. Rec. 26 September 1757. By: Robt. Hughes, Joseph Price(?), Phenibas Glover (X).

Page 139: Will of JOHN BLACKBURN of Amelia County, dated 17 July 1757, Pro. 26 September 1757. Son, William Blackburn,

land on branch of Fighting Creek; son, James Blackburn, half of
land in Albermarle county; other half to Solomon Akars, son of
Blackburn Akars after his father's death; my brother, Lembuth
Blackburn, 250 a. in Albermarle county adjoining his land whereon
he now lives, he not to debar my son James from getting timber
from it; son, William, after death of my wife or her marriage,
my negro woman; son, James, one negro woman to be bought after
my death with money due me; my wife to have use of negroes when
bought during her life or widowhood. Ex.: wife, Elizabeth and
William Maxey. Wit.: William Finny, John Gribbs.

Administration of estate of John Blackburn was granted to Elizabeth Blackburn with Joseph Bondurant and Joseph Bingley as
securities.

Page 141: Appraisal of estate of PETER LEWIS SOBLETT, dated
          26 September 1757. By: William Harris, Bennett Good,
James Holeman, Jr.

Page 142: Will of JOHN BUTLER, dated 28 February 1752. Ex.: my
          wife, Jane and Josiah Hatcher. To my wife, Jane, all
my estate. Wit.: George Benjamin Turner, Samuel Weaver, Step(?)
Robards.   John Butler (X)

Page 143: Appraisal of estate of JOHN BEAL, deceased. Ordered
          recorded 22 November 1757. By: Henry Hatcher, Robt.
Thomson, George Cox.

Page 144: Appraisal of estate of GEORGE WINNIFORD. Ordered
          recorded 23 January 1758. By: William Hopson, Wm.
Clark, Christopher Roberson (X).

Page 144: Will of ELIZABETH FLIPPEN, dated 25 September 1747,
          Pro. 23 February 175_?. My three daughters, Ann
Salle(?), Elizabeth Bedford, Sarah Goode; my six children: Ann
Salle, Elizabeth Bedford, Robert Flippen, Sarah Gunter, Thomas
Flippen, Ralph Flippen; my four grandchildren: Thomas Johnson,
Anne Johnson and John Johnson and William Johnson. Ex.: my
son-in-law, Stephen Bedford. Wit.: Wm. Taylor, Thos. Bedford,
Micajah Mosby.

          Will of ISAAC HUGHES, dated January 22, 1758, Pro.
          24 April 1758. In trust of Henry Cox, 112 a. of land
and a water grist mill, also my negro man, Major to be sold by
the said Henry twoard payment of my debts; my beloved wife during
her life and to be divided ½ to Patty Mosby and her heirs and
should there be no heirs, to her brother, George Walton, the
other half to disposal of my wife, Martha. Wit.: Stephen Cox,
Henry Farley, Geo. Walker, Anne Farley.

Page 157: Account of JAMES BARNES, by sale 9 July 1757, by
          Stephen Bedford and John Netherland.

          Inventory of estate of MICHAEL ROWLAND by Benjamin
          Cannon, Rec. 27 February 1758.

Page 149: JOHN WORLEY - will, dated 22 March 1757. Wife, Esther
          Worley; grandson, Charles Massey if he should die,
then to John Gipson, Sr.; to Thomas and Elizabeth Gibson; to John
Worley, the younger and my grandson the other plantation where
his father now lives but my son John Worley shall live on the
said plantation during his life but not at liberty to sell it
nor rent it; my son, William Worley; my daughter, Mary Maxey;

my daughter, Christian Agee; my daughter, Jude Smith; my daughter, Elizabeth Gibson. Wit.: Carrell Keon, Nathaniel Maxey.

Page 150: Appraisal of estate of ISAAC HUGHES, 24 April 1750. Recorded 22 May 1757. By: Richard Bingley(?), Robt. Thomson, Thomas Mosby.

Page 152: Will of MARY SCOTT, dated 26 December 1755, Rec. 24 July 1758. Son, Saymer Scott, all my estate. Ex.: son, Saymer Scott. Wit.: Isham Richardson, Mary Tomson (X), Gideon Anderson.

Page 153: JOHN HOLLOWAY of Southam Parish, Cumberland County, dated December 13, 1757, Pro. 24 July 1758. Son, John Holloway's three daughters, viz: Sarah, Phebe, Drucilla, 200 a. of my 500 a. land beginning on West line running on both sides of Soake Arse Creek and a negro man when they arrive at age of 18 years; my son, James Holloway; my son, William Holloway, land where he now lives; my son, Samuel Holloway, land where I live; my wife, Hannah Holloway; granddaughter, Mary Hudgens; daughter, Jane Meador; daughter, Martha Hudgens . Ex.: wife, Hannah and two sons, James and William Holloway. Wit.: John Bowden, John Hix, Charles Holand, Mary Bowden(?). Securities: James Meador and Alexander Trent.

Page 155: Account of sale of SAM'L. SCOTT, 28 August 1758, Rec. 25 September 1758. By: N. Davis, Wade Netherland.

Will of STEPHEN BEDFORD of Southam Parish, Cumberland County, March 7, 1750, Rec. 28 August 175_? (Pale). Wife, Elizabeth; daughter, Sarah Mosby; son, Benjamin Bedford; my daughter, Martha Mosby; Sarah Mosby; son, Thomas Bedford; son, Stephen Bedford. Ex.: wife, Elizabeth; friend Col. George Carrington and sons Thomas and Stephen Bedford. Wit.: Robt. McLaurine, Richd. Ligon, Joseph Harris, Chas. Clark.

Sale of BENJAMIN WOODSON.

Page 160: Appraisal of estate of JOHN HOLLOWAY, 24 July 1758. Ex.: James Holloway, William Holloway. By: Ralph Phlem...(?), William Clark, William B...(?)

Page 16_: Will of JOHN TAYLOR of Southam Parish, Cumberland County. Pro. 23 October 1757. Exrs.: son, James Taylor, friend, John Pleasants. Beloved wife, Avis Taylor; son James to have care of my negro Sill after my wife's decease during his life and to pay all my debts at that time and if any due, if not my desire is that the labour of this fellow shall be lodged in the hands of my son, James Taylor, after he is paid out of it for his board as the court shall think fit until the children hereafter mentioned be able to go to school that is Avis Moss, John Moss, John Taylor son of James Taylor, Sarah Robertson, John Taylor Ferguson, then the said money to be divided, in schooling the said children, the boys to have three years each and each of the girls 2 years each but in case Frances Amos should take away his son John Amos after my decease from his grandmother, I desire that he should have no part of my estate; remainder of money that is left after the above mentioned Children's schooling to be equally divided between Avis Amos, Martha Taylor, John Taylor Ferguson; daughter, Susannah Robertson, granddaughter, Avis Amos; two granddaughters, Mary and Sarah Robertson; daughter; Mary Ferguson; granddaughter, Martha Taylor, land where my daughter Mary lives along the Haystack Path to

Mayos line to my son James's line, thence along....to my brother, Wm.'s line. If said Martha Taylor should die without heir, I desire to return to her brother, James Taylor; grandson, John Amos, 100 acres, Capt. Mayo's and Howard's line; grandson, John Taylor Ferguson. Wit.: Wm. Taylor, Delpha Richards, Mary Taylor.

John Taylor (X)

Page 165: STEPHEN COX of Southam Parish, dated June 12, 1758. Loving brother, William Cox; loving sister, Elizabeth Clement; estate to remain in hand of executor of will till my brother Josiah arrives to age 21 then divided; to my mother, Judith Cox and my brother, Josiah Cox and my four youngest sisters, to wit: Sarah, Mary, Tabitha and Martha Cox. Ex.: Mother, Judith Cox and brother, Josiah. Wit.: Thomas Moody, Henry Farley, John Hubbard.

Page 166: Account of Sales of ROBERT WALTON, 12 June 1758. Ex.: Tucker Woodson. Rec. 22 June 1758 Court.

Page 170: Appraisal of estate of HENRY MARTAIN returned by William Womack, Henry Macon, John Woodson, William Watson. Rec. August 24, 1758.

Page 172: Account of estate of ANTHONY LE VILLAIN. By: Joseph Starkey. Rec. 25 August 1755.

Page 172: Inventory and appraisal of estate of ELIZABETH COUSINS. Returned by: Samuel Flournoy, William Harris, Peter Sobley (X). 25 September 1758.

Page 173: Sale of estate of JOEL CHANDLER, October 15, 1755. Rec. Ct. 24 February 1756. Names mentioned: Priscilla Chandler, Joseph Chandler, David Chandler, John Fleming, John Netherland, Robert Chandler, John Chandler.

Page 174: Account of estate of ROBERT WALTON, deceased. 24 April 1758.

Page 176: Inventory of estate of MARGARET RANENE(?), dated 25 September 1758. By: William Harris, Sam'l. Flournoy, Peter Sobley (X). (Note: the name is not plain, sometimes looked like Rapene.)

Page 177: 28 December 1751. Executors of estate of BENJAMIN WOODSON sold a negro woman, Jude and child named Dick to Joseph Woodson; negro man named Dick to John Woodson.

Page 177: Inventory of estate of STEPHEN COX. 27 January 1759.

Page 178: Will of NICHOLAS COX of Southam Parish, dated 1 December 1758, Pro. February 26, 1759. Grandson, Stephen Mosby, plantation whereon I now live provided my grandson Stephen Cox when he comes of age conveys unto his brother, Joseph Mosby all his right and title to the 400 a. of land whereon his father, Jacob Mosby now lives, but if he should refuse and should not make his brother, Joseph such right and title, then I give and bequeath and 400 a. to my grandson, Joseph Mosby; my two daughters Susanna Mosby and Elizabeth Mosby; grandson, Joseph Mosby, 25 lbs; grandson, Samuel Mosby, 25 lbs (under age); grandson, Robert Mosby, (under 21); grandson, Charles Mosby (under age; granddaughter, Agnes Mosby, daughter of Jacob Mosby, 25 lbs (under age); granddaughter, Phoebe Mosby, 25 lbs (under 21); grandson, Edward Mosby, 25 lbs; grandson, Daniel Mosby; grandson, Nicholas Mosby,

25 lbs (under age); granddaughter, Mary Mosby, 25 lbs (under 21); granddaughter, Sarah Mosby, 25 lbs (under 21); granddaughter, Agnes Mosby, daughter of Hezekiah Mosby, 25 lbs (under 21); grand-daughter, Susannah Mosby, 25 lbs (under 21); granddaughter, Anny Mosby, 25 lbs (under 21). Ex.: sons, Jacob and Hezekiah Mosby. Test.: Thompson Swann, Ralph Flippen, John Flippen.
Nicholas Cox (X)

Page 180: Appraisal of estate of RICHARD EPPERSON. By: Jos. Bondurant, William Maxey (X), John Cannifax. 26 March 1759

Page 181: Will of WILLIAM BOND, dated 10 October 1756, Pro. April 23, 1759. Son, Moses Bond, 250 a. land I live on; son, Philip Bond, ether loiety of land I bought of Silvanis Hill; wife, Jane Bond; sons and daughter, William Bond, John Bond, Philip Bond, Page Bond, Moses Bond, Ann Walls, Jane Holland; to my sons and daughter William, John Thomas, Edward, Wright, Philip, Page, Moses, Ann, Jane. Ex.: friend, George Carrington and my two sons, William and John. Wit.: Robert Smith, William Hughes, Edward Clements.

Page 182: Inventory of estate of MARY SCOTT, deceased. 28 May 1759.

Page 183: Will of ROBERT CARTER, dated 15 September 1753, Pro. May 28, 1759. Beloved wife; sons, Thomas Carter and John Carter, 400 a. on North side of Willises Creek; my son, Charles Carter, 329 a. land where I now live; grandson, Giles Carter, 160 a. where his father now lives after his father's decease; son, Thomas Carter, a negro boy; son, John Carter, a negro Betty; son, Charles, 12 negroes; my daughter, Susannah Carter, negro, Hannah; my grandson, Giles Carter, negro Jack after his father's decease; son, Robert Carter, 1 sh.; my daughter, Mary, feather bed and furniture; my son, Thomas, John, and Charles and my daughter, Susannah, the 2 negroes lent to my wife to be divided amongst them after my wife's decease. Ex.: sons, Thomas and Charles Carter. Wit.: John Alexander, John Rowland, John Palmore, Dan'l. Matthews.

Page 185: Account of sales of STEPHEN COX. Inventory and sales. May 28, 1758.

Page 185: Will of BENJAMIN HARRIS of Southam Parish, Cumberland County, dated 4 September 1757, Pro. 4 September 1757. Wife, Ann Harris; my children. Ex.: wife, Ann Harris and Richard Epps. Test.: Thos. Moody, William Flippen, Mary Morgain.

Page 187: Account of WILLIAM WALKER, deceased. 12 March 1759. Rec. Account and Sales. Rec. May 17, 1750.

Page 188: Estate of JOHN CANIFAX, deceased. 23 July 1759. By: William Battersby.

Page 189: Appraisal of WILLIAM BOND. May 28, 1759. By: Robert Flippen, Thos. Walker, William Holland.

Page 190: JOHN HAMMAN, SR., 30 November 1758. January 22, 1759. Son, John Hamman; daughter, Douty Coles; daughter, Agnes Hamman. Ex.: my son, Joseph Hamman, John Nelson. Wit.: John Nelson, John Hay, Warren Walker.
John Hamman

Page 191: GEORGE LOGAN, November 23, 1759, Pro. 28 January 1760.
        To Arthur Mosley of Cumberland County Parish of King
William, my crop of corn, wheat and tobacco; to Sarah Mosby,
daughter of Arthur Mosley(?). Ex.: Arthur Mosby. Wit.: George
Smith, Daniel Bunch(?).   George Logan (X)

Page 192: Estate of ROBERT EASLEY, deceased, 4 August 1759. By:
        Stephen Easley, admr. Rec. 27 August 1759.

Page 193: JAMES SMITH, 17 July 1759. To my Godson, James Smith,
        plantation I live on; to George Smith, son of Ann
Smith; to Ann Mansfield, wife of Sam'l. Mansfield, five pounds;
Ann Smith, widow of George Smith, 435 a. in Cumberland County
lying on N. Branch of Swift Creek....Ex.: James and George Smith.
Wit.: Samuel Flournoy, Stephen Forsee (X), John Forsee.
                        James Smith (X)

Page 194: Inventory of NICHOLAS COX, February 25, 1760. By:
        Jacob Mosby, Hezekiah Mosby.

Page 195: Account of estate of ISAAC HUGHES, deceased. Extrx.:
        Martha Hughes. Presented by Henry Macon, Thos. Daven-
port. 26 April 1760.

Page 196: Estate of GEORGE LOGAN, deceased, 28 April 1760.
        Appraised by: Matthew Bingley, An....? Martin, George
Smith.

Page 196: Will of FRANCIS JAMES, dated 27 July 1756, Pro. 26 May
        1760. Granddaughter, Elizabeth James as heirs at law
of my son, Francis James, deceased; granddaughter, Christina
Meredith and to her heirs, negro boy now in possession of William
Clarke; my wife, Mary James; my son, Richard James. Ex.: my
wife, Bennett Goode, Richard James and William Megginson. Wit.:
Thos. Wilkes, Wm. Megginson, Francis Maccran.

Page 197: ACHILLES BOWKER, of Southam Parish, dated 8 November
        1758, Pro. 26 May 1760. Son, Ralph Bowker; wife,
Martha Bowker; my four sons, Thomas Bowker, Achilles Bowker,
Anthony Bowker, and Bird Bowker. Exr.: wife, Martha Bowker and
my two sons, Ralph Bowker and Thomas Bowker. Wit.: William
Smith.   Achilles Bowker L.S.

Page 199: THOMAS WATKINS, dated March 4, 1760, Pro. June 23,
        1760. Daughter, ..?.. Woodson; daughter, Mary Woodson
of Goochland County; my three sons, Thomas Watkins, Joel Watkins,
and Benjamin Watkins; daughter, Elizabeth Daniel; grandson,
Stephen Watkins now living in Amelia County; to his sister,
Elizabeth; grandson, Thomas Watkins, son of my son Thomas; son,
Benjamin Watkins, land in Chesterfield County on S. Side of Swift
Creek; to daughter, Jean Watkins; grandson, Thomas Watkins, son
of my daughter, Jean Watkins; grandson, Joseph Watkins, son of
my daughter, Jean Watkins; my granddaughter, Hannah Watkins,
daughter of my son, Benjamin; my daughter, Susannah Woodson; unto
Ann Dickens, use and profits of 200 a. land during her life or
widowhood including my plantation whereon I now live....Swift
Creek. Wit.: John Watkins, Jordan Anderson, Joel Watkins.
                        Thomas Watkins

Page 200: VALENTINE MARTAIN, May 21(?), 1758, Rec. 28 July 1760.
        To my son, ..?.. Martain, 200 a. of land whereon he
now lives; son, Valentine Martain, 100 a. joining land, Besons(?)
land; son, Jobe Martain; my two sons, Samuel and Isom, land where-

on I now dwell; my John Martain, land; daughter, Ester Bond; daughter, Sarah Cunningham; daughter, Jane Boatright; my beloved wife. Wit.: Sam'l. Taylor, Davis Thompson, Samuel Bridgewater.

                                    Valentine (V his mark) Martain

Page 201: Inventory of estate of BENJAMIN HARRIS, 25 August 1760. By: Richard Epps.

Page 203: MARY JAMES, dated December 17, 1759, 25 August 1760. Daughter, Martha Clark; daughter, Phebe Merriman; son, Richard James; grandson, Francis Merriman. Ex.: Richard James. Wit.: Martha Goode, Mary Goode.   Mary James (X)

Page 206: ROBERT HUGHES, of Southam Parish, dated 21 February 1760, Pro. 27 October 1760. Eldest son, Jesse Hughes; son, Robert Hughes; son, David Hughes; wife, Ann; I leave part of my estate to fall to me at death of my mother to be equally divided between my two daughters, Francis Hughes and Martha Hughes (under 21); my wife, Ann Hughes. Ex.: my wife, Ann Hughes, David Hairfield, John Fleming, Henry Hopson. Test.: John Hughes, William Spear, John Robins, Donald McCain (X).

Page 209: Account of JOHN JOHNSON, September Court 1760. By: Joseph Johnson, one of the exors.

Page 211: Will of DANIEL MAYO, dated December 8, 1760, Pro. December 8, 1760. Wife, Mary; daughter-in-law;Francis Swinney; son, Daniel Mayo (under 21); son, William Mayo (under 21); my children during their minority; my land in Albermarle County to be sold....Ex.: my wife, Mary Mayo and my brother-in-law, George Carrington. Wit.: Thos. Montague,Thomas Hughes, Thomas Linthicum.   Dan Mayo

Codicil: mentions sons, Dan and William; daughter-in-law, Frances Swinney; wife, Ann; sister Ann Carrington's three daughters, Hannah and Mary and ..?.. Hennington; my sister, Sarah Joneses daughter, Mary; my two brothers, John and Joseph Mayo. Wit.: James Taylor, Wm. Taylor, Edmond Tony.

Page 214: Inventory of WILLIAM WILLIAMS, deceased, 3 March 1761, 23 February 1760(?). By: Stephen Mosby, Edward Mosby, Hezekiah Mosby.

Page 214: Will of ABRAHAM HUGHES, of Southam Parish, dated 10 January 1760. After the decease of my Mother, Martha Hughes, I give and bequeath an equal division betwixt J and (?) my brother Robert Hughes and to my cousin John Walton, all land which my father, Robert Hughes left me; my sister, Mary Walton. Test.: John Robinson, Thomas Poindexter, Elizabeth Hughes.

Page 215: Will of BENJAMIN HOWARD, 14 January 1761, Pro. 25 May 1761. My loving wife....(was very pale); my daughter, Anne Allen; my daughter, Elizabeth; my daughter, Lockey; my daughter, Mary; my daughter, Martha; my daughter, Rebecca; my son, Cary; my son, Benjamin. Ex.: Col. Archd. Cary. Test.: David Bell, Henry Trent, Sam'l. Allen.

Page 217: Will of CHARLES BRADSHAW, March 1761, 22 June 1761. Wife, Jemima; son, Joel; son, William (under age); son, Joel; daughter, Temperance Bradshaw; daughter, Ruth Bradshaw. Exors.: my wife, Jemima and my two brothers, William and Josiah. Test.: Field Bradshaw, John Bradshaw, Joseph

18

Robinson (R his mark).   Charles (C B his mark)Bradshaw

Proved as securities: William Hobson, John Hobson, Hezekiah
Robinson.

Page 218: JOHN SALMON, JR., dated 29 January 1761, Pro. 22 June
          1761. Wife, Eleanor Salmon; eldest son, John Salmon;
to be equally divided between my four sons, John, Lewis, Ezekiah
and Rowland; three youngest son's schooling and maintenance;
Lewis, Ezekiah and Rowland to be under their eldest brothers
care. Ex.: my wife, Eleanor Salmon and oldest son, John. Test.:
John Newton, John Salmon, Jr.

April 22, 1764. Eleanor Salmon, extrx. of will of John Salmon
was granted letters of administration - Dec. John Newton.

Page 221: Appraisal of estate of MR. BENJAMIN HARRIS, deceased.
          By: Richard Pringle, Thompsom Swann, Robert Easley.
27 July 1761

Page 223: Will of JOSEPH BINGLEY, 1760, Pro. 24 August 1760.
          Wife, Judith Bingley; my cousin, Matthew Bingley, son
of Nathaniel Bingley, 12 of land I now live on; the other half
to Joseph Bingley, "son of Edith Edwards to him and his heirs
forever...."; Matthew Bingley, son of Nathaniel, my negro girl
Hannah; to Elizabeth, daughter of David Bingley; to Mary, daughter of David Bingley; to Horatio Turpin, son of Thomas Turpin;
to Edith Edwards; to my wife, all my household goods, stocks,
cattle....Ex.: my wife, Judith Bingley. Test.: Sam'l. Flournoy,
Elizabeth Flournoy, Childress Smith (X), Robert Davis (X).
                                  Joseph Bingley L.S.

Page 224: Inventory of estate of ROBERT HUGHES, 24 August 1760.
          Ex.: Ann Hughes

Page 224: Will of JAMES HOLMAN, of Parish of King William, 7 Nov-
          ember 1760, Pro. 22 November 1760. My mother, Sarah
Holman; my wife, Jane during her life, three negroes, viz:
Jonathan, Frank and Flora and my servent, Jacob, till he comes of
age and the paying, his freedom, also my house building and war
Money; my son-in-law, Arthur Martin, one negro woman, Jude and
her future increase, my servent Boy Wall, till he arrives to....
years, he paying his freedom; son-in-law, William Martin, negro
man, Boson, servant boy Austin, he paying his freedom when he
arrives to age of 21; my son, James; my son, William; my son,
Henry; daughter, Mary; my land up in Goochland, at the discretion
of my executors, income or profits to be applied toward schooling
and clothing of my five children, viz: James, John, William,
Henry and Mary; after my mother's and wife's death, all shall be
equally divided between my seven children, viz: Sarah, Jane,
James, John, William, Henry and Mary. Ex.: my wife, Jane Holman
and two son James Holman, L.S., in law Arthur Martin and William
Martin and friend, Thomas Prosser(?). Wit.: John Bilbo, John
Martin, Daniel Perron (X).

Page 228: Will of JOHN CARLYLE of Southam Parish, 16 December
          1760. Wife, Frances, all my estate; if my wife be
with child at time of my death, then I give all estate to such
child and at his or her heir after decease of my wife. Exors.
to pay unto my Godchild, Charles Fleming, Robert Bernard, Tabitha
Harris and Samuel Easley, 10 lbs. Ex.: my wife, Frances Carlyle,
Friends, Wade Netherland, Sr., John Park, Littleberry Mosby and
my cousin, John Carlyle. Test.: Thompson Swann, Rhod. Easley.

Page 229: Will of JOHN CHASTAIN of King William Parish, 22 November 1760, Pro. 25 January 1762. Wife, Charlotte; children, John Chastain, Jr., Judith Chastain and Magdalene Chastain, eldest son, John Chastain, tract of land; son, John, negro girl; daughter, Mary Witt, wife of Benjamin Witt. Exor.: wife, Charlotte Chastain and son, John Chastain. Test.: David LeSueur, John Vilain, Chas. Clark. John Chastain L.S.

Page 232: Appraisal of estate of CHARLES BRADSHAW, deceased. Returned by: Adcock Hobson, Gideon Pat...., Sam'l Jones. 1762

Page 232: Will of JOHN SCURRY, February 12, 1762, Pro. February 22, 1762. Tract of land whereon I now live to be sold at expiration of five years for the better part and education of my children; to my son, Benjamin, tract of land after my wife, Elizabeth's death; after her death, my will is that the stock of all kinds and my furniture to be equally divided among my children....Ex.: Wife and Francis Spalding. Test.: Samuel Flournoy, James Smith, John Lookaden(?).

Page 235: Inventory of the estate of ACHILLES BASKERVILLE. By: Rhod. Easley, Jos. Woodson, Poindr. Mosby. October 20, 1760. Rec. at Court 22 March 1762.

Page 243: Appraisal of the estate of MICAJAH TURNER, 13 April 1762. Samuel Brown, William Holland, John Minter.

Page 243: Appraisal of the estate of JOHN SOLOMON. Produced by the executors: Samuel Bridgewater, John Armistead, Thomas Freeman Fretwell.

Page 244: Will of BARNET SLOVER(?), dated 6 January 1762, Pro. 24 May 1762. Wife, Catherine; son, Peter; daughter, Jane Moseley; daughter, Sarah Slover (under 18); to son, Peter, all my land except two acres and that to be sold and....thus between John Hughes, Henry Hopson, John Pleasants and William Cox, Sr. and the main road, the aforesaid 800 a. of land that I lend to my wife to return to my son, Peter, after her decease.... Ex.: wife, Catherine Stoner. Wit.: Francis Hopkins, Jane Hopkins, Thos. Wilkes.

Page 246: Will of THOMAS WOOLDRIDGE, dated 22 February 1762. Son, John Wooldridge; son, Thomas Wooldridge; son, . Henry Wooldridge; son, Henry Wooldridge, land in Cumberland County, including the plantation whereon Richard Blankenship now lives; son, David Wooldridge, 250 acres; son, Joseph Wooldridge; daughter, Frances Barker, Mary Wooldridge, Elizabeth Wooldridge, Martha Wooldridge, if any of daughters dies before she arrives to the age of 18 years....Exors.: friend, John Watkins, Thomas Watkins. Wit.: Thomas Wooldridge, Jno. Watkins, Jno. Wooldridge, Thos. Hall.

Page 247: Appraisal of the estate of JOHN SCURRY. Adm. David Ross. By: John Hobson, Adcock Hobson, Frederick Hatcher. 24 May 1762.

Page ___: Appraisal of the estate of JOHN CARLYLE, deceased. Exor.: Jno. Park. By: William Swan(?), Thomas Swan, Poin. Mosby. Rec. 25 May 1762.

Page 251: Inventory of estate of THOMAS BROWNE, deceased. 22 March 1762, Rec. June 1762. Subscribers: Job Thomas,

Samuel Atkinson, James Cunningham. Rec. June 1762.

Page 252: Inventory of the estate of THOMAS WOOLDRIDGE, deceased
           and appraisement. 23 July 1762. Thos. Hall, Israel
Winfree, Isham Akin. Rec. July 26, 1762.

Page 253: Appraisal of the estate of NOAH BAILEY, deceased.
           12 July 1762.

           Appraisal of the estate of RICHARD BROWNE. July 26,
           1762.

Page 254: Appraisal of the estate of JOHN SCURRY. Jos. Bondurant,
           James Smith, William Maxey. 23 August 1762.

Page 254: Inventory of the estate of JOHN CHASTAIN, deceased.
           29 July 1762. By: John Chastain, Charlotte Chastain.
Rec. 13 August 1762.

           Appraisal of slaves of JOHN CHASTAIN. By: John
           Vilain, John Bernard (X), Thos. Smith. July 1, 1762.

Page 256: Will of AMBROSE RANSOM, dated 29 May 1761, Pro. 23 Aug-
           ust 1762. Son, Flanstead(?), 100 acres of land; son,
Ambrose, 75 acres; son, Robert, 25 acres; son, William, 25 acres;
son, Henry; daughters, Lucy, Catherine and Jane. Exors.: son,
Flenstead Ransom. Wit.: William Angley, Jr., Christopher
Chaffin, Hambo(?) Chaffin.

           Account of sale of estate of MICHAEL ROWLAND, deceased.
           Rec. 24 August 1762. Names mentioned: Leander Daniel,
Nicholas Davis, John Rowland, Col. Shelton, Robert Carter, Samuel
Taylor, George Carrington, William Dillon, John Pleasant, Francis
Amos.

Page 258: Appraisal of the estate of AMBROSE RANSOM. 27 Septem-
           ber 1762. By: Flansd. Ransom. Returned by: Joel
Walker, Gideon Glen, Nathan Glen.

Page 237: Inventory of estate of A. BOWKER, deceased. Returned
           by Ralph Bowker. Inventory and appraisal of estate
of Achilles Bowker in Spotsylvania County was returned 21 March
1762. Thos. Steger, Wm. Hill, William Cannon(?).

Page 238: Inventory of the estate of JAMES HOLMES, deceased
           taken and appraised by: Peter Soblett (X), Robt.
Hughes, John Harris. 22 March 1762.

           Goochland County, December 3, 1762. Appraisal of
           estate of JAMES HOLMAN, deceased in Goochland County.
Presented by: Matthew Woodson, Joseph Woodson, John Woodson.

Page 241: Will of CHRISTOPHER BALEY, May 4, 1762. Son, Benjamin;
           daughter, Mary Ann Baley; son, John. Ex.: son, John
Baley. Wit.: Jacob Ashurst, Henry Moore (X), Mary Moore (X).
                                signed: Christopher Baley

Page 259: Will of PHILIP THOMAS of Southam Parish. Date....,
           Pro. 22 May 1762. Son, William; daughter, Margaret
Davis; daughter, Mary; son, George, land in Lunenburgh County;
son....(was too pale to read); son, Philip; beloved wife, Nancy
(was pale but looked like Nancy, but later says Mary); daughter,
Ann Thomas; grandson, Benjamin, son of....(was too plae). Ex.:

wife, Mary(?) and son, Philip. Wit.: Benj. Childrey, Charles Hudspeth, Mary Hudspeth (X).

Page 260: Inventory of the estate of DANIEL STONER, deceased. Taken November 17, 1762. Rec. 22 November 1762.

Appraisal of estate of RICHARD BROWN. Rec. 22 November 1762. Charles Lee, John Brown, Robert Johns

Page 262: Inventory and appraisal of estate of PHILIP THOMAS. By: Wm. Bayley, Wm. Elam, Wm. Smith. Taken 14 December 1762. Ordered recorded May 14, 1762.

Inventory of the estate of THOMAS RUSSELL. Rec. May 23, 1763. John Cox, Thos. Lockett, Edmond Watt.

Page 263: Will of JOHN HANCOCK, dated 12 March 1763, Rec. 27 June 1763. Brother, Samuel Hancock, land in....the half on which my....father, Matthew(?)....my father not to be disturbed as long as he lives; wife, Martha, land; sons, Samuel (eldest), John and William, negro girls to my three children: Ann, John and William when they come of age. Exors.: brother, Samuel and John Horton. Wit.: Thos. Redd, Wm. Penick, Pleasant Richardson.   John Hancock

Page 265: Appraisal of estate of STEPHEN DAVENPORT, deceased. Returned by: Charles Ballow. Ordered rec. August 22, 1763. William...., John Bowles.

Page 266: Inventory of the estate of STEPHEN DAVENPORT. Taken July 20, 1763. Rec. 22 August 1762. Signed by Molly Davenport.

Page 267: Inventory of the estate of ANTHONY MORGAN. By: William Cox, Jas. Bagby, John Hyde Sanders. August 19, 1763(?) Rec. 25 July 1763.

Page 268: Will of JOHN HOLLAND of Southam Parish. Date 24 July 1763, Pro. 26 September 1763. Wife, Jean; son, James, land in Buckingham County; son, Thomas, land in....300 a. I now live on; my children....Ex.: Benjamin Wilson, Jacob Winfree, Jr., James Holloway. Wit.: John Holland, James Huggins, Wm. Walls.
                                    Signed John Holland

Page 269: Will of JOHN STEVENSON, 13 April 1763, Pro. 20 September 1763. Wife and my daughter, my stock; my wife to have her choice; my daughter, Barbara....; to James Cocke Edwards, a watch; to Jacob Mosby, my silver spoons; daughters Mary(?) and Margaret, 60 pounds; to...., a choice of a guardian; mentions land on River Holstein and Clinch River in Augusta County; daughters, Janet, Barbara, Mary,....Ex.: ....and Margaret, son-in-law, James Prince, friend, Jacob Mosby. Wit.: G. Carrington, Nathan Carrington, Joseph Calland. I direct that my executors dispose of the land I bought of James Akin and the money divided as directed, as in the sale of my other estate....Wit.: G. Carrington, Nathan Carrington.

Page 271: Will of PAGE BOND, dated 29 May 1763, Pro. 26 September 1763. Wife, Ann; son, William Bond; my four children, William, Sarah, Wright, and Nancy. Ex.: William Holland, Jr., John Bond, Moses Bond. Wit.: John Holland, Samuel Holloway, John Walls.   Page Bond (X)

Page 272:   Appraisement of estate of THOMAS ELSON as produced by
            George Carrington, admr. February 9, 1760. Isaac
Berryman, Dennis McCormick, John Palmore.

Page 273:   Will of ADOLPHUS HENDRICK, dated 20 January 1762, Pro.
            24 October 1763. Son, Benjamin, 400 a. on Cair(?)
Creek; son, William; son, John; son, Moses, land on Dept Creek;
daughter, Cristina Evans; daughter, Rachel Gillentine; daughter,
Allice Hubbard; daughter, Mary Childres; two granddaughters,
Rachel Childres and Susan Childres; daughter, Betty Bostick;
daughter, Jane Robinson, negro woman named Tamar. Exors.: sons,
Benjamin Hendrick and Moses Hendrick. Wit.: Samuel Jones,
Samuel Melton, John Chumey.

Page 275:   Inventory of WILLIAM HUGHES, November 11, 1763, Court
            27 February 1764. Simon Gentry, Thomas Walker, Ralph
Flippen.

Page 276:   Inventory of estate of ROBERT WALTON, deceased. Ac-
            count returned by Executor, George Walton and examined
by: Thomas Turpin, Bennett Goode. Rec. 24 October 1763.

Page 277:   Inventory of the estate of JOHN STEVENSON, deceased.
            Saymer(?) Scott, Jas. Anderson, Joseph Michaux.
14 October 1763.

Page 278:   Appraisement of estate of JOHN HANCOCK returned and
            ordered recorded 20 November 1763. No names.

Page 281:   Appraisement of estate of STEPHEN MOSBY. John Hobson,
            Ralph Flippen, Chas. Scott. Rec. 28 November 1763.
A further appraisement was returned by Alice Onaday Mosby. Rec.
28 November 1763.

Page___: Inventory of estate of WILLIAM MOSELEY, deceased.
            Taken and appraised, 28 April 1763. Mentions estate
in Cumberland and Buckingham counties. Creed Haskins, Wm. Marshall, Frances Marshall.

Page 284:   Account of administration of estate of STEPHEN DAVEN-
            PORT, deceased. Presented to court and examined by
John Mayo and Henry Macon. Rec. 23 January 1764.

Page 285:   Will of WILLIAM HOBSON of Southam Parish, dated
            4 September 1763, Pro. 27 February 1764. Wife, Eliza-
beth; son, John Hobson; youngest son, William Hobson; daughters,
Mary, Elizabeth and....(was too pale); brother, John Hobson,
haf....built on....partnership between us....; my five children,
John, William, Mary and....(was pale but it might have been
Frances) and Elizabeth. Exrs.: wife, Elizabeth Hobson and my
brother, John Hobson, William Hobson and John Burton. Wit.:
Samuel Jones, Gideon Patteson, Jesse Merryman, Chas. Patterson,
Jr.   Signed William Hobson

Page 286:   Account of administration of estate of BENJAMIN HARRIS
            examined and ordered to be recorded 27 February 1764.

Page 288:   Appraisement of estate of PAGE BOND presented and
            ordered recorded 26 September 1763. Sam'l. Brown,
Jno. Bradley, Jno. Minter, James Holloway.

Page 288:   Appraisement of estate of JNO. HOLLAND. By: Wm.
            Holland, Jno. Bradley, Jno. Minter. Rec. Ct. 20 March
1764.

Page 289: Will of HENRY CLAY of Southam Parish, 8 March 1764;
28 May 1764. Wife, Lucy; sons, Henry, Samuel, Thomas;
slaves to fall to me after my mother's death, to my two sons,
Samuel and Thomas; to son, Masten Clay (under age); daughter,
Becky Clay; son, John Clay (under age); daughter, Lucy; son,
Elijah Clay; all my children namely Henry, Charles, Samuel,
Thomas, Obia(?), Mastin, Beckey, John, Lucy, Elijah. Exors.:
John Maxey and my two sons, Henry and Sam'l. Clay. Wit.: Thomas
Moseley, John Taylor, Abraham (A, his mark) North.

Page 298: Appraisal of estate of WILLIAM HOBSON. Returned
28 May, 1764. John Brown, Simon Gentry, Christopher
Robinson.

Page 299: Will of DOROTHY MOSS, no date, Pro. 25 June 1764. Son,
William Moss; son, Joseph Moss; Elizabeth Morriss(?);
son, John Moss; granddaughter, Elizabeth Moss, daughter of Joseph.
Ex.: sons, Joseph Moss and John Moss. Wit.: Richard Radford,
Nathaniel (M N, his mark) Maxey.

Page 295: Will of THOMAS LIGON, deceased of Southam Parish, Rec.
25(?) June 1764. Wife, Betty Ligon, 400 a. in Prince
Edward County, if my wife be with chil....I give the remainder
of my land in Prince Edward County; my sister, Elizabeth; unto
William Bailey; my brother, John Ligon. Ex.: Major Richard
Povall and my brother, John Ligon. Wit.: Richd. Eggleston,
Samuel Hopson, James Ligon.

Page 296: Appraisement of estate of PHIL DANFORD, deceased. By:
William Hobson, Christopher Robinson, Wm. Clarke.
Rec. 24 September 1764.

Page 296: Inventory of estate of JOSEPH BINGLEY. Taken at the
dwelling house by Judith Bingley and Thomas Turpin,
exors. Presented and ordered recorded by Wm. Elam, Wm. Smith,
Samuel Hobson. Ct. 24 September 1764.

Page 298: The Will of JAMES LIGON of South Parish, 25 June 1764,
Pro. 24 September 1764. Son, James, all land in
Prince Edward County; my wife, Judith; my two children, James
Ligon and his sister, Mary. Ex.: friend, Matthew Mosely, my
brother, Richard Ligon. Test.: Richard Povall, Thomas Childrey,
Joseph Moseley.   James Ligon (X)

Page 279: Will of MATTHEW LIGON of Southam Parish, date (?)April
1764, Pro. 24 September 1764. Son, James Ligon; son,
Richard Ligon. Exrs.: son, Richard - sole executor. Wit.:
Thomas Ligon, William Ligon, Frances Ligon.

Inventory of estate of HENRY CLAY returned by HENRY
CLAY, admn. Returned and ordered recorded December 22,
1764.

Page 380: Will of JOHN PLEASANTS. My Ann; son, Samuel, 130 a. I
bought of James Robinson adjoining land on which I now
live, also one tract of 50 a. I bought of Francis West, another
70 a. bought of Susanna Carna(?) both lying at the upper end of
this tract; and in case the child my wife now goes with should be
a daughter, I give unto my son, Samuel, 250 a. out of land I
bought of John Ware by consent of Thomas Jefferson on Joneses
Creek; daughter, Jane Pleasants; if the child my wife goes with
proves to be a boy, the land I bought of John Ware....Ex.: my
wife and my kinsman, James Pleasants. Lastly I appoint my dear

brother, Robert, guardian to my dear children. Test.: James
Pleasants, Judith Scott, Mary Turpin.

Court of 28 January 1765, proved by oath of Judith Scott and
affirmation of Joseph Pleasants. Ordered recorded.

Page 302: Will of MARTHA HAMBLETON of Southam Parish, dated
6 October 1758, Pro. 25 February 1765. Son, William.
Ex.: son, William Hambleton. Test.: Elizabeth Genkin (X).
Martha (M, her mark) Hambleton

Page 303: Appraisement of estate of JAMES LIGON. October 1764.
Josh Baskerville, Richard Povall, Wm. Elam. February 25, 1765.

Appraisement of estate of JAMES LIGON. October 25,
1765. Matthew...., Jacob King(?), James Hobson.

Page 306: Inventory of estate of JOHN PALMER, deceased. By:
John Toney, William Toney, Edmund Peters. 9 August
1763.

Appraisal presented December 1, 1765 by John Carter,
John Norton(?), John Armistead. Rec. April Court 1766.

Appraisal of estate of DAVID THOMPSON. Returned by:
Job Thomas, Martin Richardson, Phis, Thomas. Rec.
22 April 1766.

Page 30_: Will of JOHN WATKINS, dated November 1764. My beloved
wife, Phebe; son, John; son, Samuel; son, Henry,
daughter, Mary Moseley; daughter, Sarah Porter; daughter, Rachel
Watkins; daughter, Phebe Watkins; daughter, Betty Watkins; my
four sons, John, Edward, Samuel and Henry; I desire my children
may be maintained and schooled, out of my estate, my 7 children,
John, Edward, Samuel, Henry, Rachel, Phebe and Betty. Ex.:
friend, Thomas Pross to have the directing and dividing of my
land between my three sons, Edward, Samuel and Henry agreeable
to my will and as he shall think most convenient for the benefit
of my children. Ex.: my wife and my son, John Watkins. Wit.:
John Watkins, Tho. Watkins, Samuel Warinner, Abraham Baugh.

Codicil: 31 December 1764. The remainder of my estate that I
have not given away but lent unto my wife Phebe and after her
decease to be equally divided between my 7 children my desire is
that my wife may dispose of as she sees fit.

Page 310: Appraisal of estate of JOHN PLEASANTS late of Cumberland County taken 26th March 1765. Rec. 21st March
1765. Thos. Turpin, Sam'l. Flournoy, Wm. Flournoy.

Page 305: Appraisal of estate of JOHN PLEASANTS. Returned and
ordered recorded 28 October 1765.

Page 313: Inventory of estate of JNO. WATKINS. Recorded 28 October 1765.

Page 315: Will of HUMPHREY SMITH, dated 15 February 1766. Proved
23 June 1766. Wife, Judey Smith. Ex.: wife, Judey
Smith. Wit.: William Maxey, Tho. Hall, John Maxey.

Will of BENJAMIN POINDEXTER of Southam Parish, 28 December 1765, Pro. 23 June 1766. To my friend, Little-

berry Mosby and Joseph Carrington, everything I possess, as the
heirs I was to have by my wife Ann Poindexter as her legacy and,
lastly I do appoint as exrs.: Littleberry Mosby and Joseph Carrington. Wit.: James McDowall, Thos. Caldwell, John Watts (X).

Page 305: Appraisal of estate of JOHN ROBINSON. By: John Hughes,
          Nicholas Formby, Henry Flippen. Pro. 25 August 1766.
One old feather bed and furniture, an old sack bag and wearing
apparel, a remnant of...., some old pewter and knife and fork,
two small grind stones, parcel of...., 2 bushels of...., a parcel
of old books, an old Casket, piece of bacon, old work bence, some
beeswax, one chest of desk and books, some walnut plants.

Page 306: Account of administration of estate of JAMES LIGON.
          Rec. 25 August 1766. Thomas Turpin, Richard James.

Page 317: Will of JOHN FORSEE, dated 28 August 1766, Pro.
          27 August, 1766. Brother, Stephen Forsee, my four
brothers, Stephen, Francis, Charles and William Forsee; my sister
Mary Ann Maxey. Ex.: Samuel Flournoy, Judith Bingley. Test.:
Thomas Bradley, William Bradley, Thomas Vawter.

Page 318: Appraisal of estate of JOSEPH FRANKLING, deceased.
          Returned December 8, 1766. By: Simon Hughes, David
Parker, Robt. (R, his mark) Douglas. Court 22 December 1766.

Page 318: Appraisal of estate of JOHN LINCH, deceased, and inven-
          tory taken by John Scott and returned. December 8,
1766. Court 22 December 1766.

Page ___: Appraisal of estate of RACHEL TEVERS. John Carter,
          John Armistead, Samuel Allen. Rec. 25 February 1767.

Page 320: Inventory of estate of COLLINS JOHNSON, deceased by
          David Terrell, John Jones, John Matlock. 16 May 1766,
rec. 23 February 1767.

Page 321: Will of THOMAS PORTER, of King William Parish, 15 April
          1765, Rec. April 1767. Wife, Elizabeth; son, John
Porter; son, William Porter, land I purchased of Peter Bilbo;
son, Isaac Porter, to have two years schooling; son, John and
William to have equal division of land on Joneses Creek; daughter,
Sarah Hatcher, land in Albermarle County, daughter, Ann, land in
Albermarle County; daughter, Mary; my children, John, William,
Isaac, Elizabeth, Sarah, Ann and Mary. Ex.: wife, Elizabeth and
two sons, John and William. Wit.: Thos. Prosser, John Shelton,
Chas. Woodson, Jr., Samuel Warinner.

Page 325: Will of JOHN FLEMING, April 1763, Pro. 27 April 1767.
          In compliance with injunction laid on me by my father,
John Fleming, I devise to my brother, Charles, parcel of land on
Willises Creek....; beloved wife, Susanna(?); son, John; also to
my wife, two lots in Gatesville in Chesterfield County; son, John
my violin I bought of Col. Hunter; I appoint my brothers, Thomas,
William and Richard guardians to my son, John M. and my wife
guardian to my daughters. Ex.: my son, John when he shall attain
to age of 21 and my brother, Thomas, William and Richard. Test.:
Thomas Fleming, Wm. Fleming.

Page 325: Will of JOHN HOLT, 20(?) October 1766; 27 April 1767.
          Wife, Tabitha Holt; daughter, Betty; if the child my
wife is now with shall be a son, to share with brother and sister;
unto Happy, daughter of Mary Turner of the county of Caroline.

Ex.: Robert Lumpkin of King and Queen County and my wife. Test.: John Barnes, John...., Nathaniel Johnson (X).

Page 326: Appraisal of estate of JOHN HOLT, 29 April 1767; 25 May 1767. William Howard, John Chandler, Balt Stovall.

Page 317: Account of administration of estate of JOHN SALMON, Eleanor, 22 June 1767. By: Geo. Carrington, N. Davies

Page 328: Will of JAMES HARRIS, dated 24 May 1767, Or. 27 July 1767. Wife, Sarah, tract of land whereon I now live; son, Thomas Harris, after the expiration of five years from date hereof, the upper part of plantation whereon I now live....including all the land between the said line of Benjamin Harris and on the death of his mother or her marrying again I then give my said son, Thomas the rest and residue of my plantation and the tract of land I now live on including land I bargained with Jesse Sanders but have not yet a conveyance for to him and my said Thomas and his heirs forever but in case a title to said land bought of Sanders should not be obtained by my son, then my will is that the money I was by bargain to give for the same being 500 lbs. to be equally divided among my five sons: Thomas, John, William and Francis; to daughter, Phebe Farrar; to daughter, Mary Harris; my four youngest sons, James, John, William and Francis; "lands in Buckingham and Chesterfield counties" to sons James and John. Exrs.: my wife, my son Thomas and my brothers, Benjamin Harris and William Harris and my friend Samuel Flournoy. Wit.: John Vilain, Thos. Smith, John Bransford, Jr.

Page 331: Inventory of the Estate of THOMAS PORTER, deceased, returned by Elizabeth Porter, John Porter, Jr., exrs. Dated May 28, 1767, Pro. May 28, 1767.

Appraisal of estate of WILLIAM EVANS. Returned and approved at a court by: Jas. Begby, Daniel Johnson, Jas. Johnson. 27 July 1767

Page 332: Appraisal of estate of WILLIAM LIGON. Returned 26 October 1767 by: Richard Ligon, Samuel Hobson, Geo. Radford.

Page 333: Appraisal of estate of CARTER DAVIS. Appraisal returned by: Jacob Michaux, John Hughes, Jas. Bagby. Administrator: John Cox. Court 26 October 1767.

Page 333: Will of CHARLES BALLOW of Southam Parish, dated 18 May 1767, Pro. 23 November 1767. Wife, Temperance; son, William, daughter, Anne Ballow, negro boy Jammey that is now at her grandfather Bailey's and my negro girl Amey when she shall be of age; son, Charles Ballow, land I bought of Richard Daniel on Appomattox River in Cumberland County; son, Jesse (under age); son, John; daughter, Mary Ballow. Ex.: son, Charles Ballow, Thomas Prosser, Edward Hoskins and Alex. Trent. Wit.: James Dowdie, Jr., Thos. Davenport, Jr., John Burton.

Page 335: To all to whom it may concern, know ye that I Temperance Ballow widow of Charles Ballow, deceased, do hereby declare that I will not accept or take the legacy to me given or bequeathed or any part thereof of my said husband in and by his last will and I do renounce all benefit which I might claim by such will. In witness whereof I have hereunto set my hand and seal. Recorded 22 February 1768. Wit.: Francis Amoss, Simon Rowland, G. Carrington.

Page 335: Inventory of estate of JOHN FORSEE, deceased. By:
          Sam'l. Flournoy, Judith Bingley. November 21st, 1767.
Rec. 23 November 1767.

Page 336: Appraisal of estate of CHARLES HOLLAND. Returned by:
          Samuel Holloway, John Bradley, James Holloway, Wm.
Allen. Rec. 22 February 1768.

Page 336: Will of JOHN LE VILLAIN of King William Parish, dated
          26 January 1765, Pro. 22 February 1768. Wife, Phillipe
LeVillain, free use of all land whereon I now live in the Manna-
kin town also use of 120 a. in Chesterfield County that I pur-
chased to Nath'l. Finch; daughter, Elizabeth Woodson. Ex.: wife,
Phillipe, John James Dupuy and my son-in-law, Matthew Woodson.
Wit.: Wm. Porter, Jr., Jane Chastain, Chas. Clarke.

Page 336: Will of JUDITH WALKER, dated 19 August 1767, Pro. 1768.
          Daughter, Lucy LeGrand; daughter, Judah Perry(?);
granddaughter, Judah LeGrand; son, Benjamin Walker; son, Henry
Walker (under 21); to sons, Warren Walker and Benjamin Walker;
to son, James Walker; son, Joel Walker; son, William Walker; son,
Peter Walker; cash, a crop to be divided among sons, viz: James,
Warren and Joel, and Peter and William by Matthew Nelson and
James Allen. Ex.: son, William Walker. Wit.: Matthew Nelson,
John Owen, Mack Goode.   Judah Walker (X)

Page 339: Account of administration of estate of JOHN FORSEE by
          Sam'l. Flournoy and Judith Bingley. Examined and
ordered recorded. Returned October 26, 1767. Account examined
by Thos. Turpin and Thos. Turpin, Jr. November 25, 1767. Rec.
22 February 1768.

Page 340: Will of JOHN HYDE SANDERS, dated February 2, 1768.
          Pro. 29 March 1768. My wife in lieu of her dower all
my estate in confidence that she will maintain and educate all
my children provided she give each their part as soon as they
come of age; son, Samuel Hyde Sanders (under age); sons, Robert
and Chancellor Hyde; sons, Jesse and John Hyde, land on little
Deep Creek which is now in their possession; son, Peter Sanders,
195 a. whereon he now lives in Pettsylvanis County; daughter,
Rebeccah Sanders; daughter, Mariana Sanders. Exrs.: friends,
William Fleming, Archibald Buchanan, and my son, John Hyde Sanders. Wit.: James Taylor, Daniel Johnson (X), Bart Stovall,
Jr., John Frankling (X).

Page 341: Will of JOHN JOHNSON, dated 14 January 1768, Pro.
          March Court 1768. My sons, Daniel, John, James,
Jeremiah be bound out to trade at the discretion of my exrs.;
son, Daniel, my plantation whereon I now live, 75 a.; son, John,
100 a. whereon Elsabeth Evins now lives; son, James, remaining
part; son, Jeremiah, 50 lbs. when he comes of age; wife, Sarah
Johnson, my plantation and all the rest of my estate but 1 bed
and furniture as long as she lives, the other bed and furniture
to be sold; to my daughter, Mary, 50 lbs. when my estate is sold
or when she come of age or marries; to daughter, Phebe, 40 lbs.
when she comes of age or when she marries; remaining part to be
divided between my 4 sons before mentioned after paying for my
children's sufficient schooling. Exrs.: Daniel Johnson, John
Hyde Sanders, Jr. Wit.: Jas. Bagby, Rebeccah Sanders, Polly
Sanders.

          Appraisal of estate of JOSEPH FRANKLING, November 1,
          1767. By: Peter Fitzpatrick, Wm. Graves, Valentine

Winfree (X). Rec. 28 March 1768.

Page 343: Will of JOHN ROBINSON, dated 11 December 1767, Rec.
          28 April 1768. My four grandchildren, John Roberson,
Susannah Roberson, Elizabeth Roberson and Joseph Roberson, my
negro man Jack to be divided among them when said grandson, John,
comes of age and till then he the said negro Jack to be under the
care and direction of my son, Joseph Roberson for support of my
four grandchildren above named; my sons, John, Thomas, Field,
Christopher, Edward, Joseph and Hezekiah, a shilling sterling
they having received their equal part out of my estate; to my
three daughters, Susannah Bradshaw, Judith Bradshaw and Elizabeth
Hogan, all the rest of my estate to be equally divided between
them only 7 lbs. which has already been paid William Bradshaw,
my will allow 2/3 of that money out of her part of my estate, to
the other two namely Judith Bradshaw and Elizabeth Hogan. Ex.:
son-in-law, Field Bradshaw, son-in-law, William Bradshaw. Wit.:
Adcock Hobson, Hezekiah Robinson, William Robertson, Joseph
(R, his mark) Robinson.   John (R, his mark) Roberson

Page 334: Giles Driver was called on to prove non-cupative Will
          of THOMAS RUSSELL, deceased. 18 September 1761. He
swore that Thomas Russell in his last sickness at the house of
Francis Marshall's where was taken sick signified his desire
that William Marshall should write his will, his wife - brother,
Peter Russell - to have his mare which was then at Francis
Marshalls and his land and allotted the money due him from Capt.
Haskins, and that at the time of the said Russells making this
declaration he was residing at the said Francis Marshalls above
10 days and that he particularly called on the said Giles to
taken notice of his....At a Court held 23 November 1761 Mary
Marshall being called on and proved this will swore that Thomas
Russell on his death bed signified his desire that William Marshall or John Cox should write the will but neither coming in
time declared to the said Mary that he desired his brother Peter
should have his land and mare and that the said Thomas desired
her to take notice of this declaration. She also heard him say
he had six pounds in Capt. Haskins hand which must go to dis-
charge his funeral expence.

Page 346: Joseph Palmer, Martha Reynolds, Sr. and Martha Rey-
          nolds, Jr. swore to the noncupative will of JOHN
PALMER, deceased. His wife, Cicely Palmer; three sons. Ex.:
George Carrington, Jr. 25 July 1763

Page 346: Edmund Clements and Robert Douglas, Jr. swore to non-
          cupative will of WILLIAM HUGHES, deceased. 24 Oct-
ober 1763. ....that he desired Simon Hughes to keep his estate;
mother and daughter together until daughter should want it.
Letters of administration were granted to Simon Hughes.

Page 346: Account of administration of estate of HENRY CLAY. In
          list of names mentioned were: Jno. Mosely, guardian
to Obia Clay; Geo. Hancock, guardian to Martin or Masten Clay;
legacies to Thos. and Sam'l. Clay; Lucy Clay; Richd. James;
Israel Winfree; Ben Hatcher; Chas. Hatcher; Francis Cheatham;
Wm. Marshall; Thos. Hall; Thos. Lockett; Wm. Mosely. By: John
Mayo and Thomas Swann. Examined and ordered recorded March 1768.

Page 347: Inventory and appraisal of estate of JOHN ROBINSON,
          deceased. Items listed: 30 head of cattle, head of
hogs, 1 young horse, 1 cart, 1 negro man Jack, parcel of plantation tools, 2 plows and gear, saddle and bridle, parcel of leather,

29

old chest and old chairs, 1 parcel of pewter, 1 spice mortar and
pestle, 1 parcel of knives and forks, earthen ware, 1 pot, parcel
of old delft ware, 2 iron pots, parcel of old casks and water
vessel, 2 old meal...., 1 pair old fire tongs, 1 parcel of old
lumber, parcel of salt, parcel of corn, parcel of tubbs. Sworn
to 30 April 1768. John Hobson and Wm. Clark. Ordered recorded
23 May 1768.

Page 351: Inventory and appraisal of JOHN JOHNSON, 27 June 1768.
By: George Owen, James Bagby, Anthony Minter.

Page 352: Inventory and appraisal of estate of JOHN HYDE SANDERS,
27 June 1768. By: George Owen, James Bagby, Anthony
....

Will of ANN SMITH, dated 15 February 1761, Pro. 25 July
1768. Grandson, George Smith, oldest son of Thomas
Smith, 10 pounds; granddaughter, Mary Ann Mansfield; granddaughter
Elizabeth Mansfield, 10 pounds; son, James Smith's daughters; two
sons, James and George Smith; estate to be equally divided be-
tween them. Ex.: two sons, James and George Smith. Wit.:
Thomas Bradley, Wm. Bradley, Stephen Forsee, Joan Forsee (X)
Ann Smith (X)

Page 355: Will of PETER ANTHONY LOOKADO, dated 5 November 1767,
Pro. 25 July 1768. Son, Peter Lookado; daughter,
Judith; wife, Elizabeth; 4 daughters, Mary Ann Agee, Elizabeth
Cary(?), Rebecca Thomas, Judith Lookado. Exrs.: my wife and my
friend Thomas Thomas. Wit.: Sam'l. Flournoy, James Smith,
Joseph Salle.

Page 350: Inventory of estate of JUDETH WALKER. Ex.: William
Walker. Presented and ordered recorded at Court
25 July 1768.

Page 356: Will of WILLIAM MAXEY of Southam Parish, dated 27 May
1768, Pro. 22 August 1768. Son, John, 400 a. whereon
I now live; my daughter, Jemimah Maxey; daughter, Keziah Maxey;
Keren Heppuek Salle; Edward Maxey, son of Silvanus; my grandson,
William Davis, son of George; Jeffrey Davis, son of George Davis;
my loving wife, Mary; my five daughters. Exrs.: my two sons,
John and Nathaniel Maxey. Wit.: Thomas Haskins, James Holloway,
Jos. Bondurant.   William (W, his mark) Maxey

Declaration of Mary Maxey against the will.
Mary Maxey, relict of William Maxey dissatisfied with the provision of her husband for her by his will made declaration that
"I for myself and my heirs executor and administrator renounce
all Benefits and advantages of my late husband to which I might
claim by virtue of such late will and declare I will not accept
or take any of the legacys to me therein given insisting on
receiving such part of said estate as the law has provided for
me.... Wit.: Sam'l. Flournoy, Jos. Bondurant, Thos. Haskins.
Rec. 22 August 1768.   Mary Maxey (X)

Page 359: Inventory and Appraisal of JOHN GILLIAM, deceased, by
Jacob Mosby, Jos. Mosby, Benj. Bedford. Recorded
Court 22 August 1768.

Will of ORLANDO HUGHES of Southam Parish, dated
25 July 1768, Pro. 26 September 1768. Wife, Elizabeth; two youngest sons, Josiah and Anthony; son, Caleb; son-in-
law, John Murray. Ex.: son-in-law, John Murray and my son,

30

Leander. Wit.: William Howell, Micajah Hughes, Josiah Hughes.

Page 360: Inventory of Estate of WILLIAM MAXEY, deceased. Exrs.:
           John Maxey, Nathaniel Maxey. Court 26 September 1768.

Page 361: Will of JONAS MEADORS, SR., dated 5th May 1768, Pro.
           22 August 1768. Son, Jessey, 200 a. land whereon I
now live; son, John; son, Jehu; son, Joab; wife, Frances. Wit.:
Michael Jones, Thomas Adams (X), Mary Ann Adams (X).
                              Jonas Meador (X)

Page 362: Appraisal of WILMOTH WINIFORD. By: William Hobson,
           Adcock Hobson, Frederick Hatcher. Rev. November 28,
1768 Court.

Page 363: Account of admin. of FRANCIS JAMES, JR. August Court
           1760.

           Account of admin. of estate of ELIZABETH JAMES, orphan
           of Francis James. Examined August 24, 1752.

Page 362: Appraisal of WILMOTH WINIFORD.

Page 364: Account of administration of estate of JOSEPH JENKINS,
           orphan by John Hubbard, his guardian. 24 August 1750.

           Account of administration of estate of JOHN BARNES,
           orphan by Mary Barnes.

           Account of administration of estate of JAMES BARNES,
           orphan by Mary Barnes. Examined and approved August
1752.

           Account of administration of estate of FRANCIS BARNES,
           orphan by Mary Barnes.

           Account of administration of estate of MARTHA BARNES,
           orphan by Mary Barnes, ex.

Page 366: Account of JOSEPH GINKINS (JINKIN) by John Hubbard,
           guardian. 27 August 1763.

Page 366: Account of administration of estate of ELIZABETH JAMES,
           orphan.

           Account of administration of estate of FRANCIS JAMES,
           JR. Account returned by Francis James and ordered
recorded September 24, 1753.

Page 367: Account of administration of estate of MARY BARNES,
           orphan of James Barnes by Mary Barnes, guardian.
Examined and ordered recorded September Court 1753.

Page 367: Account of Guardianship of GEORGE BARNES, orphan of
           James Barnes by Mary Barnes, guardian. September
Court 1753.

Page 368: Account of guardianship of JOHN BARNES, orphan of
           James Barnes by Mary Barnes. September Court 1753.

Page 368: Account of guardianship of MARTHA BARNES, orphan of
           James Barnes by Mary Barnes, ex. and ordered rec.
September 20, 1753.

Page 369:   Account of guardianship of JAMES BARNES by Mary Barnes
            examined and ordered rec. September Court 1753.

Page 369:   Account of FRANCIS BARNES, orphan of James Barnes,
            deceased, returned by Mary Barnes, examined and order-
ed rec. September Court 1753.

Page 370:   MARY BARNES, orphan of James Barnes, account returned
            by guardian, Mary Barnes. Examined and ordered re-
corded August Court 1754.

            MARTHA BARNES, orphan of James Barnes, deceased pre-
            sented by guardian, Mary Barnes, August Court 1754.

Page 371:   FRANCIS BARNES, orphan of James Barnes presented and
            approved at August Court 1754.

Page 372:   JAMES BARNES, orphan of James Barnes, deceased, pre-
            sented by Mary Barnes. Approved at August Court 1754.

Page 372:   JAMES BARNES, orphan of James Barnes, account present-
            ed by Mary Barnes at August 22, 1755 Court.

Page 373:   FRANCIS BARNES, orphan of James Barnes presented by
            Mary Barnes and approved at August Court 1755.

Page 373:   Account of GEORGE BARNES, orphan of James Barnes pre-
            sented by Mary Barnes and approved at August Court 1755.

Page 374:   MARTHA BARNES, orphan of James Barnes, account pre-
            sented by Mary Barnes and approved at August Court 1755.

Page 375:   FRANCIS BARNES, orphan, account of estate presented
            and ordered recorded August Court 1755.

Page 376:   Account of MARGARET BERNARD presented by Nathaniel
            Davis and examined and ordered recorded August Court
1755.

            JAMES BARNES, orphan of James Barnes, account present-
            ed by Mary Barnes. Rec. September Court 1756.

Page 378:   JAMES BARNES, orphan of James Barnes presented by Mary
            Barnes.

Page 378:   MARY BARNES, orphan of James Barnes, deceased, pre-
            sented by Mary Barnes. September court 1756.

Page 379:   MARTHA BARNES account presented and rec. September 1756.

Page 379:   MARGARET BERNARD account presented by Nathaniel Davis
            examined and ordered recorded September Court 1756.

Page 380:   MARY BARNES, orphan of James Barnes, account presented
            by Joseph Crampton. August Court 1757.

Page 380:   MARTHA BARNES, orphan of James Barnes, account pre-
            sented by Jos. Crampton. August 22, 1757.

Page 381:   FRANCIS BARNES, orphan of James Barnes by John Barnes.
            August 20, 1757.

            JAMES BARNES, orphan of James Barnes to John Barnes.

August Court 1757.

FRANCIS BARNES, orphan to James Barnes. August Court 1758.

Page 382: Estate of ANTHONY LE VILLIAN, deceased in account with John LeVillain, guardian. August Court 1756.

Page 383: Estate of MARY LE VILLAIN, orphan of Anthony LeVillain in account with John LeVillain. August Court 1757.

Page 384: MARY LE VILLAIN, orphan of Anthony LeVillain in account with John LeVillain, guardian. 20 August 1758.

Page 385: MARY BARNES, orphan to James Barnes in account with Joseph Crampton. September Court 1758.

Page 386: MARY LE VILLAIN, orphan of Anthony LeVillain in account with John LeVillain, guardian. August Court 1759.

Page 387: Account of administration of HENRY WALKER, orphan of William Walker, deceased, in hands of Warren Walker. August Court 1759.

Account of administration of BENJAMIN WALKER, orphan of William Walker, in hands of Warren Walker, guardian. August Court 1759.

Account of JUDITH WALKER, orphan of William Walker, in hands of Warren Walker, guardian. August Court 1759.

Page 388: Orphans of JOHN HOLLOWAY, deceased, to Daniel Hogan for clothing and boarding of orphans 9-3-3.

Account of administration approved January Court 1760.

Page 388: Account of estate of FRANCIS BARNES by John Barnes. September Court 1759.

Page 370: Account of administration of estate of ROBT. WALTON, orphan by Robt. Walton. Examined and approved January Court 1760.

Page 370: Account of estate of JOSEPH JENKINS presented and approved at August Court 1758 by Joseph Hubbard, his guardian.

Account of administration of estate of MARGARET BERNARD presented by Nicholas Davis, guardian. August Court 1758.

Page 392: Account of estate of MARGARET BERNARD presented by Nicholas Davis. August Court 1759.

Account of estate of MARGARET BERNARD presented by Nicholas Davis. August 25, 1760.

Page 393: Orphan of ANTHONY LE VILLAIN, deceased, in account with John LeVillain. August Court 1760.

Page 395: Account of estate of FRANCIS BARNES by John Barnes, guardian. August Court 1760.

JOSEPH JENKINS, orphan of John Jenkins, deceased, account of administration presented by Joseph Hubbard, guardian. August Court 1760.

JAMES HUDGENS account presented by William Hix, his guardian. August Court 1760.

Page 396: SARAH, PHEBE, and DRUCILLA HOLLOWAY, orphans of John Holloway in account with Daniel Hogan, their guardian. Among items mention: August 25, clothing and boarding orphans; credit, rent from plantation, January 21 to August 25. January 1760, hire of a negro. Account approved August Court 1760. (Note by KR. This must have been the plantation left them.)

Page 396: List of slaves in possession of George Walton, guardian of SALLY WALTON which said slaves are to be equally divided between Sally Walton by their father's will besides which I have in the estate of Robert Walton in my possession. Sworn to by John Hughes, guardian. 22 September 1760.

Page 396: SALLY WALTON, orphan of Robt. Walton by guardian, Geo. Walton. September Court 1760.

Page 400: JOHN WALTON account by Tucker Woodson. Among items listed as expenses was board at Robert Hughes. September Court 1760.

Page 401: MARTHA JOHNSON, orphan of John Johnson in account with Joseph Johnson, guardian. September Court 1760.

Page 401: JOSEPH JENKINS, orphan of John Jenkins account returned by Joseph Hubbard, guardian. August 24, 1760.

Page 401: SARAH, PHEBE and DRUCILLA HOLLOWAY, orphans of John Holloway in account with Daniel Hogan, their guardian. Among expenses were clothing and boarding from August 25, 1760 to August 24, 1761 and also rent of Plantation (credit). Hire of negro. August Court 1761.

Page 402: Estate of ANTHONY LE VILLAIN in account with John Le Villain, orphan guardian to Mary LeVillain orphan of said Anthony; expenses and credits. August 21, 1761.

Page 403: MARTHA JOHNSON, orphan of John Johnson by Joseph Johnson. August 1761.

Page 403: ROBERT WALTON, orphan of Robt. Walton to Martha Hughes for one months board and to Robt. Hughes, taylor for making one suit of clothes. Received money due from George Walton. Paid Robt. Walton on account. Account returned by John Hughes. August Court 1761.

Page 404: Account of administration of estate of ELIZABETH JAMES, orphan by Richard James. August 17, 1761.

Page 406: Account of administration of estate of SALLY WALTON by George Walton. August Court 1761.

Page 406: George Walton as guardian to JOHN WALTON makes statement he has received unto his care of his estate one negro man named Toby, that he has hired out for 12 pounds and one tract of land and plantation on James River computed at 130 a. which he has rented out for seven pounds ½ of the quit rents and tax of the repairing of the house thereon....Date 18 August 1761.

Page 408: MARGARET BERNARD account of administration returned by N. Savis August 21, 1761. Account of administration was presented by Nicholas Davis and Margaret Bernard signed statement that this account and all others had been settled to her satisfaction except her negroes and some cattle which were to be delivered to her order before next....September Court 1761.

Page 408: GEORGE WALTON, orphan of R. Walton, deceased, by Geo. Walton returned and ordered recorded August Court 1762.

Page 409: Estate of ANN HOMESLY by Stephen Mosby. (One item was recording mother's will.) September Court 1761.

Page 410: MARY LE VILLAIN, orphan of Anthony LeVillain account returned by her guardian John LeVillain. One item was: to Joseph Starkey for 7 years boarding of Mary LeVillain and schools. August Court 1762.

Page 411: JOSEPH JENKINS, orphan of John Jenkins account by guardian, Joseph Hubbard. August Court 1762.

JAMES HUDGENS, orphan in account with William Allen, guardian. August Court 1762.

Page 412: ELIZABETH JAMES in account with Richd. James. August Court 1762.

Page 412: WILLIAM REYNOLDS account returned by John Beyley, guardian. August Court 1762.

Page 142: MARTHA JOHNSON, orphan of John Johnson. Guardian, Jos. Johnson. August Court 1762.

Page 143: MARY BARNES, orphan of James Barnes, deceased, account of administration returned by Francis Barnes. August Court 1762.

Page 412: GEORGE OTEY account returned by William Prosser. October Court 1762.

Page 414: SARAH, PHEBE, and DRUCILLA HOLLOWAY, orphans, account of administration returned by guardian, Daniel Hogan. Board and schooling, rent of their plantation. November Court 1762.

Page 414: JOSEPH JENKINS account returned, examined and ordered recorded. Joseph Hubbard, guardian. August 1763.

Page 414: Estate of ANTHONY LE VILLAIN in account with John Le Villain.

Page 146: GEORGE WALTON, orphan by Geo. Walton, guardian. August 1763.

JOHN WALTON, orphan of Robt. by Geo. Walton. August 22, 1763.

MARY, LEWIS and JOHN TURNER in account with Jonas Meadors. December 1762. 340 lbs. pork; barrel of corn; 3 yards of cotton; 3 felt hats; 1 pair shoes, etc. Account sworn to by Jonas Meadors. August 22, 1763.

JOSEPH JOHNSON, guardian to WILLIAM JOHNSON, orphan of John....by Joseph Johnson. August 22, 1763.

Page 416: JAMES HUDGENS, orphan of Jno. Hudgens, in account with Wm. Hix. August Court 1763.

Estate of WM. HUDGENS, orphan of John Hudgens in account with William Allen. 22 August 1763.

MARY HUDGENS in account with Robt. Hudgens her guardian. Sworn to by Robert Hudgens ex. and recorded September 26, 1763.

SARAH, PHEBE, DRUCILLA HOLLOWAY, orphans of John Holloway, deceased, account returned by Daniel Hogan, guardian. September 26, 1763.

Page 419: Account of administration of estate of DANIEL SANDERS returned by James Brown, guardian. 24 October 1763.

Page 420: Account of administration of estate of ANTHONY LE VILLAIN by John LeVillain. Among items listed was expenses to Mary LeVillain. August 27, 1764.

Page 421: Account of administration of estate of JAMES HUDGENS, orphan of John Hudgens by William Hix. August 27,1764.

Page 421: WILLIAM REYNOLDS, orphan of Wm. Reynolds, deceased, account returned by Jno. Bayley, guardian. August 27, 1764.

DANIEL WOOLDRIDGE, orphan of Thos. Wooldridge, account made by Richd. Parker, Jr. 27 August 1764.

Page 422: Account against estate of JOSEPH WOOLDRIDGE estate, "not any satisfaction received nor any part of his estate received." Mary Wooldridge, guardian. This account was examined and approved by the Court and sworn to by Mary Wooldridge. 27 August 1764.

Page 422: Account of administration of OTEY (no other name) by William Prosser. August 27, 1764.

DANIEL SAUNDERS, orphan in account with James Brown. August 27, 1764.

NANCY SAUNDERS, orphan of Richard Saunders, deceased, in account with Thos. Montague. 27 August 1764.

Page 423: Account of MARY, LEWIS and JOHN TURNER, orphans of Micajah Turner, deceased with Jonas Meador. One item of expense was "to boarding 3 children 1 year." 27 August 1764.

WILLIAM MOSS, orphan of Wm. Moss, deceased, in account with Bartholomew Stovall, Jr., guardian. August 27, 1764.

WILLIAM HUDGENS, orphan of Jno. Hudgens in account with William Allen. Paid his 1/3 part of his father's estate. Account examined and recorded 24 September 1764.

Page 424: MARTHA JOHNSON in account with Jos. Johnson, guardian. 24 September 1764.

Page 424: Orphans of John Holoway. Boarding and clothing SARAH,
          PHEBE and DRUCILLA HOLLOWAY for 1 year, by Daniel
Hogan. 22 October 1764.

Page 424: WILLIAM MOSS, orphan of William Moss in account with
          Bartholomew Stovall, Jr. August 26, 1765.

Page 424: MARY HUDGENS, orphan of John Hudgens, deceased in ac-
          count with Robert Hudgens, her guardian. 26 August
1765.

Page 425: WM. HUDGENS, orphan of John Hudgens, deceased in ac-
          count with William Allen, his guardian. 26 August
1765.

          WILLIAM RENNOLDS, orphan of William Rennolds in ac-
          count with John Riley, guardian. 26 August 1765.

          HENRY WOOLDRIDGE, orphan of John Wooldridge in account
          with John Wooldridge. 26 August 1765.

Page 426: Account against JOSEPH WOOLDRIDGE estate by Mary Wool-
          dridge, guardian. 26 August 1765.

          DANIEL SAUNDERS, orphan of Richard Saunders in account
          with James Brown, his guardian. 26 August 1765.

          DANIEL WOOLDRIDGE, orphan of Thos. in account with
          Francis Cheatam, his guardian. September 23, 1765.

          MARTHA JOHNSON in account with Joseph Johnson, her
          guardian. September 23, 1765.

Page 427: MARY CLOUGH, orphan in account with Richd. Eggleston,
          guardian. 23 September 1765.

          MARY, LEWIS and JOHN TURNER, orphans of Micajah Turner,
          deceased, in account with Jonas Meador, Jr., their
guardian. Paid Wm. Holloway by bond against your father's estate,
was one item in account. 28 October 1765.

Page 428: WM. MOSS, orphan of Wm. Moss, deceased, in account
          with Bartholomew Stovall. 25 August 1766.

          WILLIAM HUDGENS, orphan of Jno., deceased in account
          with William Allen. 25 August 1766.

          MARY CLOUGH in account with Richd. Eggleston. Sworn
          to and examined and recorded 25 August 1766.

Page 429: MARY TURNER, LEWIS TURNER and JOHN TURNER, orphans of
          Micajah Turner, deceased, in account with Jonas
Meador, Jr., their guardian. 25 August 1766.

          NANCY SAUNDERS by her guardian, Thomas Montague.
          25 August 1766.

Page 431: MARTHA JOHNSON, orphan of John, deceased, in account
          with Joseph Johnson. 24 November 1766.

          OBIA CLAY, orphan in account with John Mosby or
          Moselye. 24 August 1767.

WILLIAM MOSS, orphan of Wm. Moss in account with
Bartho. Stovall, Jr. 24 August 1767.

Page 431: DAN WOOLDRIDGE, orphan of Thomas Wooldridge in account
with Francis Cheatham, his guardian. 24 August 1767.

Page 432: JOSEPH WOOLDRIDGE, orphan of Thomas Wooldridge in account with Nicholas Robertson, his guardian. 24 August 1767.

JOHN WOOLDRIDGE in account with Henry Wooldridge,
orphan of Thomas Wooldridge, deceased, sworn to by
John Wooldridge and ordered recorded August 24, 1767.

Taxes on 300 a. for 1766 sworn to by Sam'l. Branch.
24 August 1767.

Page 433: MARY CLOUGH in account with Richd. Eggleston. Sworn
to and ordered recorded August 24, 1767.

DAVID SANDERS gives receipt to James Brown for 6 pounds
19 sh. 3 pence in full for his guardianship for me.
24 August 1767. Wit.: Thomas Tabb.

PHEBE, SARAH and DRUCILLA HOLLOWAY in account with
Joseph Robinson and Hezekiah Robinson. Account
approved 24 August 1767.

REBECCA CLAY, orphan in account with Thos. Clay.
24 August 1767.

MASTEN CLAY in account with George Hancock, his guardian. Sworn to and ordered recorded 24 August 1767.

NANCY SAUNDERS by her guardian, Thomas Montague.
24 August 1767.

Page 435: MARY, LEWIS and JOHN TURNER, orphans of Micajah Turner
in account with Jonas Meador, Jr. In list of items:
paid Hannah Holloway by bond against father's estate. September 28, 1767.

WILLIAM REYNOLDS in account with John Bailey, orphan
of William Reynolds. 22 August 1765.

DANIEL WOOLDRIDGE in account with John Wooldridge.
August 22, 1768.

Page 426: HENRY WOOLDRIDGE in account with John Wooldridge.
22 August 1768.

JOSEPH WOOLDRIDGE in account with Nicholas Robertson.
22 August 1768.

SARAH and DRUCILLA HOLLOWAY, orphans of John in account with Joseph Robinson and Hezekiah Robinson.
August 22, 1768.

JOHN CLAY in account with John Maseley. 26 September
1768.

Page 427: ROBERT WILLIAMSON, orphan in account with Creed Haskins. Examined and ordered recorded 22 August 1768.

MARY CLOUGH, orphan in account with Richard Eggleston. Sworn to and ordered recorded. 26 September 1768.

Page 438: MAY MOSS in account with John Moss, guardian. 22 August 1768.

Appraisal of estate of CHRISTOPHER CHAFFIN by: Nathan Glenn, Warren Walker, William Owen. 23 January 1769.

Page 439: FRANCES STEGAR of Southam Parish, dated 14 January 1769, Pro. 27 February 1769. Son, Samuel Stegar and his heirs forever, plantation whereon I now live and all the land in the said tract known by name of James Rober....; my executors to sell all my lots in Richmond town; wife, Ann Jannett; daughter, Keturah King Mariana, under 21. Ex.: son, John Parrett Stegar, son, Thomas Stegar, son, Hanes Stegar. Wit.: Littleberry Mosby, Robt. Smith, A. Davenport. Memo: The words interline ("and his heirs forever) were acknowledged by the testator after signing the above before us. T. Swann, Jas. Bryden and Jacob Mosby.

Page 440: Will of JOEL LOCKETT, dated...., Pro. 27 February 1768. Wife, Mary; 4 sons, Royall, Pleasant, Daniel and Benjamin; daughter, Fankley(?); my two youngest daughters, Mary and Elizabeth Lockett. Exrs.: Thomas Moseley, James Hankla(?). Wit.: Arthur Moseley, Robt. Haskins, John Northcutt (X).
                    Joel Lockett

Page 44_: JOHN ARMISTEAD of Southam Parish, dated 21 October 1768, Pro. 27 March 1769. Son, William Armistead; son, John Armistead; son, Francis Armistead; daughter, Sarah Russell; daughter, Elizabeth Bradshaw; daughter, Hannah Armistead; daughter, Nancy Armistead; daughter Fanny Armistead; son, Thaddeus Armistead; wife, Hannah. Exrs.: son-in-law, Josiah Bradshaw and son, William Armistead. Wit.: Samuel Atkinson, G. Carrington. By: Josiah Bradshaw and Wm. Armistead. Sec.: Field Robinson and Hezekiah Robinson, Samuel Allen.

Page 443: Will of WILLIAM HOLLAND of Southam Parish, dated 24 February 1768, Pro. 27 March 1769. Sons, John Holland, son, Spearman Holland, land (200 a. I bought of James Holloway); daughter, Ann Hubbard, 200 a. whereon she now lives; daughter, Charlotte Holland; wife, Margaret Holland. Ex.: wife and Robert Smith and James Holloway. Wit.: Thomas Adams (X), Cathron Holloway (X), Mary Brown.

Page 447: Will of WILLIAM BASSAM, dated 3 April 1768, Pro. 23 May 1768. Wife, Sarah; son, William, 200 a. whereon I now live; son, Jeremiah, 150 a. out of aforesaid tract; daughter, Sarah, 50 a. out of aforesaid tract; at decease of my wife, my whole estate to be divided among my children and grandchildren. Exrs.: sons, William and Jeremiah and my wife. Wit.: Simon Chaffin, Thomas Huckbey, Jno. Alex Steel.
                    William Bassam (X)

Appraisal of estate of WILLIAM BASSOM. By: W. Womcack, Nathan Glen, Daniel Allen. 27 June 1768.

Page 448: Inventory of estate of JOHN PETER LE VILLAIN taken by John Jas. Dupuy, Matthew Woodson. 27 June 1768.

SARAH and PHEBE HOLLOWAY in account with Hezekiah Robinson and Joseph Robinson. Examined and approved. 25 August 1766.

Received of Joseph Hubbard, guardian for me, 27 pounds, 10 shillings in full for years rents of land which is in his hands during his guardianship. August 15, 1766.

Signed by: Joseph Jenkins

THOMAS HOLLAND, orphan of John Holland in account with Ben Wilson. Some of the items: pd. Wm. Allen for clothing and schooling, rent of 300 a. land. 25 August 1766.

HENRY WOOLDRIDGE, orphan of Tho. Wooldridge in account with Jno. Wooldridge. 25 August 1766.

DAN WOOLDRIDGE, orphan in account with Francis Chatham. August 1766.

Estate of THOMAS WOOLDRIDGE in account with his guardian. Sworn to by Samuel Branch and ordered recorded. 22 September 1766.

Page 444: Will of WILLIAM MARSHALL of Southam Parish, dated 2 October 1768, Pro. 27 March 1769. Wife, Lucy Marshall, my plantation on Fighting Creek and 4 negroes, Joel, Stephen, Eady, Sall, 20 barrels corn, 600 lb. pork, etc. to support her family the one year after my death, also one feather bed and furniture which she brought with her in lieu of her right of dower; son, John Marshall, tract of land, 350 a.; son, William, land and plantation whereon I now live, 300 a., also 140 a. in Chesterfield county on Turkey Branch; my three children, John, Elizabeth and Ann should have a part of the bed and furniture I am now possessed with; all my estate not mentioned to be divided between my ten children, that is viz.: John, William, Elizabeth, Ann, Phebe(?), Mary, Tabitha, Sarah, Martha, Susannah when my son William shall come to age. Appoint Frances Marshall, Edward Bass, guardian to my children. Ex.: Thomas Worsham, William Archer and Henry Moody. Wit.: Dancey Macram, Abner Lockett, Joseph Taylor.

Page 445: Codicil: I desire that my friend, George Hancock shall be joint guardian to my children and their estates with Edward Bass and Francis Marshall and that my son, William be taught to read, write and cypher as is needful for common business and my daughter, Martha and Susannah be taught to read and write, the money for school to be paid out of my estate. Codicil rec. court 27 March 1769.

Page 445: Will of WADE NETHERLAND, dated 28 June 1764. Daughter, Frances Harris(?), 5 pounds; grandson, Wade Netherland (under 21); whereas previous to the marriage of Mr. Tucker Woodson with my daughter, Mary, and in consideration thereof I had agreed with her to settle on her 8 slaves, in such manner that the said Tucker Woodson and my daughter, Mary, his then intended wife, during there natural lives and the survival of them should enjoy the use of said slaves with all the profit from the labors of said slaves during the term aforesaid and then after the expiration of the said term then to children of such union and if no children, to my son, Wade Netherland; to Mary Lightfoot, orphan of Jno. Lightfoot, deceased, who was brother to my late wife. Ex.: son, Wade Netherland. Wit.: Thos. Fleming, Wm. Fleming.

Wade Natherland L.S.

Page 445: Inventory of estate of ORLANDO HUGHES, 24 April 1769. By: Thomas Walker, William Terrell, Ralph Flippen.

Additional inventory of ORLANDO HUGHES. 24 April 1769.
John Murray, Leander Hughes.

Page 449: Will of STEVEN CRUMP, dated 24 April 1769. Wife, Jean
Crump. Ex.: wife, Jean Crump and Robert Brown.

Page 450: Account of administration of estate of JOHN HANCOCK
with Martha Hancock. Among items mentioned: 1763
maintenance of 4 small children one year; 1764 maintenance of
4 small children one year; 1766 on tern schooling of children.
Account examined and approved 23 November 1768.

Page 450: Account of administration of estate of JOHN HANCOCK.
Some names mentioned: Joel Walker, James Anderson,
David Anderson, Leander Hughes, Sam'l. Cawter, Richd. LeGrand,
Seymore Scott, Samuel Phillips, Paid Capt. Anderson, John Holeman,
Mary Richardson, Isham Richardson, Lewis Bond. Account of admin-
istration of estate of John Hancock made by Martha Hancock, John
Morton and Samuel Hancock. Examined by Charles Anderson and
Joseph Calland and ordered approved and recorded 22 May 1769.

Page 452: Appraisal of estate of FRANCIS STEGAR. By: Chas.
Scott, Jesse Miller, Edward Tabb. 22 May 1769.

Page 453: Will of DAVID LE SEUER, JR. of King William Parish,
dated 29th February 1769, Pro. 26 June 1769. Father,
David LeSeuer; brother, Chastain LeSeuer; brother, Samuel; brother, Martell LeSeuer; brother, Peter LeSeuer; my money left me
by my grandfather in England; sister, Catherine Tompson; sister,
Elizabeth LeSeuer. Ex.: my father, David LeSeuer. Wit.:
William Harris, Francis Chastain, John Huckaby.

Page 453: Inventory of estate of JOEL LOCKETT. Taken by Thomas
Mosby and James Hankla. Approved 26 June 1769.

Settlement of estate of JOHN HOLLAND, late of Cumberland County with Benjamin Wilson, executor of said
estate. Names mentioned: William Wells, 1/9; Thomas Davenport,
27/; Thomas Holland, 35/; William Anderson, 23-11-4; Jonas Meador,
L 2-2-3; Joseph Carrington, L 3-7; John Minter, 9/; Charles May,
13-7-/; James Minter; Alexander Trent for bondage; Jacob Winfree,
Jr. to part of his account; Wm. Walker and T. Swann; Benjamin
Wilson for Thomas Holland, orphan; Benjamin Wilson for James
Holland, orphan; Credits from James Carrington for sundries,
from Wm. Allen, Wight Bond, John Daniel, Jos. Hughes, Robt. Hud-
gen, Samuel Holloway, James Hudgens, Chas....., Jonas Meador,
Jos. Merryman, John Merryman, Sam'l. Powell or Povall, Christo-
pher Robinson, Wm. Sampson, Simon Gentry, Wm. Wells, Isaac Win-
free, Wm. Holland, Jr., from Jane and Wm. Holland, Benj. Wilson,
Thos. Tabb, Benj. Wilson. From crop of tobacco sold by Jacob
Winfree, from sundries sold Jane Holland, from sundries sold
Anne Holland. Dated December 6, 1768. App. 26 June 1769 by:
Francis Tabb, Alex Trent.

Page 453: Will of RICHARD PEMBERTON, date 30 January 1769, Pro.
24 July 1769. Wife, Frances; my children, William,
Martha, James, Richard, George, Mary and Magdalene. Ex.: friend
James Briant, James Briant, Jr. Wit.: Sam'l. Flournoy, William
Bradley, John Briant.   Richard Pemberton (X)

Will of RANDOLPH JOHNSON, date 2nd April 1768, Pro.
24 July 1769. Daughter, Mary Johnson; daughter,
Elizabeth Johnson; son, Job Johnson, land in Albermarle County;

son, Randolph Johnson; son, Thomas Johnson; daughter, Rebecca Johnson; loving wife, Mary. Ex.: wife, Mary Johnson and son, Job Johnson. Wit.: Adcock Hobson, John Brown, Joanna Hobson.

Randolph Johnson (X)

Page 451: Inventory of estate of JAMES HARRIS, July 22, 1769.
By: Mary Harris, Wm. Harris, Sam'l. Flournoy. Rec. 24 July 1769.

Page 453: Will of JOHN COLQUIT, date 15 January 1769, Pro. 24 July 1769. Son, Anthony Colquit; son, John Colquit and his wife Betty; son, Johnathan Colquit; son, James Colquit; grandson, John Scruggs; daughter, Ann Scruggs; granddaughter, Sarah Scruggs; daughter, Lorresia; son, Hezekiah Colquit; granddaughter, Mary Ann Haws Colquit under 21. Exrs.: two sons, Johnathan and Hezekiah Colquit. Wit.: Thomas Nash, Lucy Nash, William Hobson.

Page 460: Inventory of estate of RANDOLPH JOHNSON. Returned and approved 28 August 1769 by: Thomas Nash, Josiah Thomas, Frederick Hatcher.

Inventory of estate of WILLIAM MARSHALL. Taken May 8, 1769 by: John Cox, Arthur Moseley, Jr., Edward Haskins. Approved 28 August 1769.

Page 461: Will of SAMUEL WEAVER of King William Parish, dated 16 December 1763, Pro..... Sons, Daniel, Samuel, John, Jesse, Joseph, David and Benjamin Weaver; three daughters, Elizabeth, Raunaux(?), Mary Dravin(?), Sarah Chastain. Ex.: son, Daniel Weaver. Wit.: J. Pleasant, Jr., Wm. Street, Richard West.

Signed Samuel Weaver

Page 462: Account of administration of estate of JOHN HOLT, with Robert Scruggs administrator. Account examined and approved 28 August 1769. L. or S. Mosby, Wm. Smith.

Page 1: ISAAC ALLEN, date 28 January 1769, Pro. 25 September
         1769. Son, Joseph Allen, land containing 280 a. adj.
land of William Coleman on Soakas Creek; land whereon I now live
to my two sons, William and Stephen containing 400 a. on South
side of Great Guinea; sale of stock and household goods and all
land, my plantation utensils after my debts is paid to be equally
divided betwixt all my children. Exrs.: my sons Drury and
Joseph. Wit.: William Arnall (X), William Faris, Jr.
                                Isaac Allen (X)

         Further inventory of estate of WILLIAM MAXEY made by
         John and Nathaniel Maxey. 25 September 1769.

Page 2: Will of JOHN MERRYMAN, JR., date 2 August 1769, Pro.
         25 September 1769. Wife, a chil's part of my estate;
son, Allen Murray, all the land I have on the South side of Muddy
Creek and a child's part of my personal estate and if my son
should die without heir, that land to be equally divided between
my daughters; to my daughter, Phebe, equal part of my personal
estate; to daughter, Polly, equal part of my personal estate; my
desire all my land on South side of Muddy Creek to be sold to
satisfie my executors but in case they will not stay while it is
sold, may be laid out to be advantage....; negroes to be equally
divided amongst my children. Ex.: wife and friends Samuel
Povall and John Jefferson. Wit.: William Costilo Hill, Joseph
Hicks, ...Merryman.   Signed John Merryman

Page 3: Appraisal of estate of EDWARD MOSBY by Ralph Flippen,
         Chas. Scott, Absalom Davenport. 23 October 1769.

Page 3: Will of JAMES DAVIS, date 6 December 1769, Pro. 22 Jan-
         uary 1770. My 200 a. in Prince Edward County to be sold
and my just debts paid out of the money and the rest of the money
that the land getches to be equally divided between my two sons,
Robert and Charles; to my son, James, 1 sh.; to my granddaughter,
Elizabeth, one table, one cow and calf and one small table; to
my son, George, 224 a. and the tract on which he now lives, and
likewise all the rest of my estate. Ex.: son, George Davis.
Wit.: Jos. Bondurant, Thos. Haskins, William Blackburn (X).
                                James Davis (X)

Page 4: Will of DANIEL COLEMAN of Southam Parish, date 29 August
         1763, Pro. 22 January 1770. Grandson, William Coleman,
son of my son, Thomas; my wife, Patience Coleman, all the land
whereon I now live containing 300 a., etc.; to daughter, Ann
Glenn and her husband, Nehemiah Glenn, negro woman now in possession of Nehemiah Glen; daughter, Lucy Glen and her husband,
Nathaniel Glen; daughter, Mary Sims and her husband, Matthew Simms;
grandson, Gideon Edwards, all my lands in Halifax County; all my
children that is to say my sons Thomas, Daniel, and James and my
daughters, (Judith Turner, deceased, part to be equally divided
between all her children), my daughter, Sarah Guthery, Ann Glen,
Grissel Edwards, Lucy Glen and Mary Simms. Ex.: son, Daniel
Coleman, Nathan Glen and Wm. Coleman. Wit.: Thos. Davenport,
Jr., William Davenport, James Davenport, Josh Davenport.

Page 6:   Account of estate of sales of RANDOLPH JOHNSON, deceased
          by Job Johnson exor. Among buyers were: Mary Johnson,
Job Johnson, William Allen Burton, John Smith, Joseph Calland,
John Lawton. Present and app. 26 February 1770.

Page 7:   Appraisal of estate of RICHARD PEMBERTON by: John Jas.
          Dupuy, James Smith, Stephen Forsee (X). February 24,
1770.

Page 7:   Will of MARTHA HUGHES of Southam Parish, dated 8 Septem-
          ber 1769, Pro. 26 March 1770. My daughter, Martha Wal-
ton; my three children, George Cox, Henry Cox and Martha Walton.
Ex.: my two sons, George Cox and Henry Cox. Wit.: Henry Cox,
Jr., Edward Walton, Jeremiah Parker.

Page 7:   Appraisal of estate of DANIEL COLEMAN. By: Samuel
          Allen, Thomas Guthrey, Moses Hudgens. Examined and
approved April 23, 1770.

Page 9:   Appraisal of estate of MARTHA HUGHES. By: William
          Allen Burton, Gideon Patterson, Frederick Hatcher. Taken
26 March 1770. Court 23 April 1770.

Page 8:   Will of ROBERT SMYTH of Southam Parish, dated 18 March
          1768, Pro. 23 April 1770. Wife, Sarah Smyth otherwise
Clemonds, all my estate; my son, Thom Smyth, all my land only
and everything thereunto belong to be divided amongst the rest
of my children share and share alike, but in case my wife remain
unmarried, I leave all in her power until death then the land to
fall to my son, Thomas, if in case son, Thomas died before his
mother, I leave the land to rest of my children. Ex.: my dear
son, Edward Elements. Wit.: James Brown, John Clemons.

          Will of RALPH FLIPPEN, dated 6 February 1768, Pro.
          28 May 1770. Son, John Flippen; son, Francis Flippen;
daughter, Jane Flippen; daughter, Elizabeth Flippen; daughter,
Mary Flippen; son, Philip Flippen; son, Robert Flippen; son,
Jacob; my wife, Martha Flippen. Ex.: my wife and son, Francis
Flippen. Wit.: Geo. Carrington, Wm. Flippen, Robert Walton.

Page 12: Will of SAMUEL ALLEN, dated 28 May 1769, Pro. 28 May
          1770. Son, Samuel Allen; daughter, Elizabeth Armistead;
son, Jesse; daughter, Tabitha Allyn; son, George Allyn; child
wife is now big with, if a daughter, bed and furniture and equal
part with my sons, Jesse, Martin, James and George, and if a son
to have equal part with my four sons. Ex.: my wife and James
Moss. Wit.: Luzey Hudgens, James Hudgens.

Page 13: Appraisal of estate of SAMUEL ALLEN. By: Samuel
          Atkinson, Martin Richardson, Jonas Meador. Examined
and approved 23 July 1770.

Page 14: Inventory and appraisal of Estate of WILLIAM HOLLAND.
          By: Simon Gentry, Edward Robertson, Simon Hughes.
Taken May 8, 1769. Examined and approved 23 July 1770 Court.

Page 16: Will of ARTHUR MOSELEY, dated 16 December 1769, Pro.
          23 July 1770. Son, Charles, son, John, land in Buck-
ingham County; son, William, land in Chesterfield County, where
my son mother now lives; son, Benjamin, land on Indian Quarter
branch in Cumberland County; son, Edward, land whereon I now
live; daughter, Prudence Moseley; my wife, remaining part of my
estate not already willed away during her life, she to have whole

estate until the children come of age or marries; my three youngest sons, William, Benjamin and Edward. Ex.: my wife, Mary and
sons, Arthur, William and Benjamin. Wit.: Richard Moseley,
Gideon Lockett, Wm. Moseley.

Appraisal of estate of ISAAC ALLEN by Henry Mason, Mark
Andrews, Joshua Doss. Examined and approved 24 September 1770.

Page 18: Will of JOHN REYNOLDS of Southam Parish, dated 21 March
1760, Pro. 22 October 1770. Wife, Mary; two sons,
Charles and Obediah; my children, Cicely, Charles, Mary, Martha,
Sarah, Obediah, Ann and Susanna; land where my mother now lives
lying in New Kent County after her death to be sold and divided
amongst my children. Ex.: my wife, Mary and son, Charles Reynolds and Samuel Taylor. Wit.: John Salmoms, Benjamin Ferris
and Elizabeth Reynolds (X).

Page 20: Appraisal of estate of ROBERT SMITH. By: Simon Gentry,
Edward Robinson, James Daniel, September 1, 1770.
Examined and approved 26 November 1770.

Will of WILLIAM DAVIS of Southam Parish, date 14 July
1768, Pro. 25 February 1771. My beloved wife, Elizabeth, plantation whereon I now live to maintain my children with
me now living under age; son, William Davis, 50 a. where Thomas
Morgan formerly lived between Charles Woodson land and my land
mortgaged to John Pleasants. Ex.: my wife and son, William.
Wit.: James Taylor, William Davis (X), Peter Davis (X).

Appraisal of estate of WILLIAM FLIPPEN. By: John
Newton, ...Martin, Phinebas Glover (X). 24 December
1770.

Page 23: EDWARD MC GEHEE'S will, dated 4 April 1770, Pro. 28 Jan-
uary 1771. Son, John McGehee, land in Prince Edward
County; daughter, Mary Hodnett; daughter, Elizabeth Wright, land
being part of tract whereon I now live and adjoining land of
Thomas Wright, Charles Lee and Frances Apperson; son-in-law,
Thomas Wright; son, Micajah McGehee; son, Mumford McGehee; son,
Jacob McGehee, 700 a. in Prince Edward County; son, William, land
in Prince Edward County; son, Samuel, negro boy; daughter, Anna
McGehee; wife, Elizabeth, land and plantation whereon I live.
Ex.: wife, Elizabeth McGehee and son, Mimford and son-in-law,
Thomas Wright and Henry Macon. Wit.: Nathan Glenn, James Glenn
and Nehemiah Glenn.

Page 25: Inventory of estate of ARTHUR MOSELEY. Taken by Arthur
Moseley the ex. 18 January 1771.

Page 26: Appraisal of estate of JOHN REYNOLDS. By: Joseph
Price, Samuel Atkins, Orson Martin, Job Thomas. Made
December 29, 1770. Approved 25 March 1771.

Page 27: Will of EDWARD WATKINS of Southam Parish, date 21 June
1765, Pro. 21 March 1771. Son, John Watkins, daughter,
Martha; two grandsons, John Clay and Edward Clay; son-in-law,
Francis Mosby; daughter, Mary Anderson; daughter Judith Bass;
two sons, John and Edward; two grandsons, Edward Watkins and
Samuel Watkins; son, Edward; son, Thomas; son, John. Ex.: two
sons, Thomas and Edward Watkins. Wit.: Thos. Prosser, Mark
Taylor, Francis Cheatam (X).   Edward Watkins (X)

Page 29: Appraisal of estate of FRANCIS AMOS. Made by: Wm.
        Lawless, John Carter, Thomas Car(?). Examined and
ordered recorded 26 March 1771.

Page 30: Appraisal of estate of JOHN WELCH. Made by: G. Carring-
        ton, Jas. Carrington, Nath. Carrington. Examined and
approved 25 .... 1771.

Page 31: Inventory of estate of WILLIAM DAVIS. Taken 20 March
        1771 by: George Owen, Robt. Scruggs, Nathan Chaffin.
Court 21 March 1771.

Page 32: Appraisal of estate of JOHN SMITH. By: Henry Macon,
        Daniel Coleman, William Daniel. Court 22 April 1771.

Page 33: Appraisal of estate of RALPH FLIPPEN. Made by: David
        Parker, Simon Gentry, Chas. Scott. Court 22 April 1771.

Page 34: Will of WILLIAM MC GEHEE, date 13 March 1771. Daughter
        Ann; child my wife now carries; land in Charlotte
County to be sold; wife, Catherine McGehee. Ex.: wife, my
brother, Jacob McGehee and friend Frederick Hatcher and Thomas
Carter. Wit.: Isham Bradley, Adcock Hobson.
                                William McGehee L.S.

Page 36: Appraisal of estate of GEORGE SEIZER. By: John Hughes,
        David Coupland, Henry Bagby. Court 24 June 1771.

Page 35: Appraisal of estate of BENJAMIN GRESHAM. By: Geo.
        Wright, Charles Anderson, Saymore Scott. Court 22 July
1771.

Page 36: Appraisal of Estate of GEORGE SEIZER. Taken by John
        Hughes, David Coupland, Henry Bagby. Court 26 June 1771.

Page 37: Appraisal of Estate of WILLIAM MC GEHEE. Taken 25 June
        1771 by: Adcock Hobson, Thomas Nash, Josiah Thomson.
Examined and approved 22 July 1771.

Page 37: Will of RICHARD POVALL of Southam Parish, dated 6 Jan-
        uary 1771, Pro. 22 July 1771. Wife, Tabitha; three
sons, John, Charles, and Richard; daughter, Betty Howlett, daughter, Mary Povall; daughter, Ann Povall; daughter, Polly Povall;
daughter, Susanna Povall; daughter, Judah Povall. Exrs.: Thomas
Prosser and my son-in-law, Samuel Hobson and Arthur Moseley, Jr.
Wit.: Thomas Childrey, Richd. Eggleston, Charles Lewis, Jr.
                                Signed Richard Povall

        Account of administration of LITTLEBERRY MOSBY. Names
        included: Chas. Easley, Ben Mosby, James McDowell,
Henry Macon, Jno. Netherland, Chas. Caldwell, James Aimen, Col.
Tabb, Jno. Wayles, Alex. McCaul for Glasgow Ingraham and co.,
John Park for sundries bougt at sale, Josiah Thompson and Wm.
Clark, Jesse Carter and Tucker Woodson, William Sampson, Miller
Dogett, Poindexter Mosby, Thompson Swann, Dan'l. Mosby, John
Cardwell, John Philip, Thos. Tabb, Frederick Hatcher, Dan'l.
Carter, Wm. Smith, Ben Mosby, Rhod. Wasley, Hezekiah Mosby, Geo.
Carrington, Patience Thompson, James McDowell, Wm. Stamps.
Account examined and ordered recorded by Wm. Smith, Robert Smith.
Certified 19 August 1771. Settlement returned and recorded
26 August 1771.

Page 41: Will of PATIENCE COLEMAN of Southam Parish, dated
          18 July 1771, Pro. 26 August 1771. Daughter, Ann Glenn;
daughter, Grissel Edwards; grandson, William Coleman, son of my
son, Thomas; son, Thomas Coleman; grandson, Gideon Edwards; great
grandson, Elliott Gulls or Grills(?) Coleman; granddaughter,
Patience Terry Syms; three grandsons, Daniel, Gulielmus and
Parmenus Coleman, sons of my son, Thomas Coleman, sum of money to
be applied toward their schooling; sons, Daniel and James Coleman;
my daughters, Sarah Guttery, Lucy Glenn and Mary Syms. Exrs.:
Nathan Glenn and William Coleman. Wit.: George Barker, John
Chatten, Rebecca Barker.   Signed: Patience Coleman L.S.

Page 43: Will of BENNETT GOODE, dated 1 October 1771, Pro.
          23 September 1771. Wife, Martha, plantation whereon I
now live and use of land adjoining, beginning at a new marked
pine on Deep Creek; to my wife, slaves Sizer, Mary, Dinah, Cloe,
Hanton, and Asher. I desire that she divide the among my children
as she thinks proper; to son, John, the plantation and land admin-
istered before and lent to my wife being the same I now live on
and after the death of my wife; to son, Bennett, tract of land I
bought of Capt. John Bailey and part of my other land joining to
it; to son, Thomas, land adjoining land I have lent to my wife
and given to my son, John; son, William, parcel of land which
lives below my son John's new line; son, William, parcel of land
laid on North Side of Deep Creel road and Michaux Ferry and joining line of Davis Sizer, John Hughes, Peter Stoner or Hanes(?)
and my son, Thomas upper line; daughter, Mary Saunders, negroes
not allotted to be divided among my sons, John, Bennett, Thomas,
William and my daughters, Martha, Alice, Elizabeth, Lucy, Sally.
Desire that Richard Liggon, Jacob Michaux, Joseph Mayo and John
Hughes divide my negroes equally among my children. Exrs.: my
two sons, John Goode and Bennett Goode and John Hughes. Wit.:
John Bailey, John Bailey, Jr., Thomas Bailey.

Page 43: Will of JACOB AMMONETTE, dated 20 August 1771, Pro.
          23 September 1771. Daughter, Mary Ann Ammonette, all
my land in Chesterfield County on Falling Creek and lying between
my brother William Ammonette and Andrew Ammonett and all the rest
of my estate but if my daughter, Mary Ann, should die without
issue, I give the above mentioned land to John Ammonett, Jr., son
of my brother, John Ammonett. Exrs.: John Woodson, Jr., Aaron
Butler.   Jacob Ammonette (X)

Wit.: John Raine, Thos. Davenport, Jr. At a court 25 September
1771 presented by executors John Woodson, Jr. and Aaron Butler.
Securities: John Holeman and Wm. Shepherd.

Page 46: Will of MARY MAXEY, of Southam Parish, dated 20 May
          1771, Pro. 28 October 1771. Son, Nathaniel Maxey;
daughter, Jamima Salle; Edward Maxey, son of Sylvanus Maxey; two
daughters, Bede Maxey and Kezia Maxey. Exrs.: Joseph Salley and
Edward Maxey, Jr. Wit.: Benjamin Bondurant, John Epperson, Jos.
Bondurant.   Signed: Mary Maxey (X)

Page 47: Appraisal of Estate of PATIENCE COLEMAN. By: Samuel
          Allen, Daniel Allen, John Burton. October 26, 1771.
Examined and ordered recorded 15 November 1771.

Page 47: Inventory of estate of EDWARD MC GEHEE. By: Elizabeth
          McGehee and Thomas Wright. Inventory exhibited and
approved 25 November 1771.

Page 48: Will of DAVID LE SEUER of King William Parish, dated

25 November 1771, Pro. February 24, 1772. Son, James LeSeuer, land in Buckingham County provided he pay my son, Peter, 50 pounds and if he refuses, the land to be equally divided between him and Peter; son, Peter LeSeuer; son, Chastain LeSeuer and Samuel Le Seuer, land in Buckingham County to be equally divided; son, Fell LeSeuer, 200 a. adjoining James' land; my son, Mantell LeSeuer, 200 a. at his mother's death whereon I now live; daughter, Elizabeth; my wife, Elizabeth; son-in-law, Robert Thompson. Ex.: my wife, Elizabeth and sons, James, Chastain and Samuel LeSeuer. Wit.: Thos. Smith, George Smith, Daniel Guerrant, Chas. Clarke.

Page 49: Appraisal of estate of JOHN WRIGHT. By: Charles Anderson, John Woodson, Jr., Joseph Michaux. Examined and approved 27 March 1772.

Page 52: Inventory of estate of RICHARD POVALL. Taken 27 January 1772. By: Samuel Hobson and Arthur Moseley. Rec. 27 March 1772.

Page 52: Will of ALEXANDER MOSS, date 10 February 1772, Pro. 27 April 1772. To Tom Tommas, 30 a. whereon he now lives likewise it being part of land whereon I now live and likewise I give him two days in every week to labr in for the maintenance of his wife and children to have and to hole the said land during his natural life and then to return to my grandson, Alexander Duiguid; to my grandson, Alexander Duiguid, remainder part of my tract of land and plantation whereon I now live after decease of my daughter, Ann Duiguid, likewise slaves; to my grandson, George Duiguid, that part of my farm and moiety and house and woodland lying in Great Brittain which I am now possessed with, also 50 pounds money when he comes to 21 and if he cannot get right to estate in Great Brittan, he is to have equal part of my estate with rest of my children except Alexander Duiguid to have and hold to him and his lawfully begotten heirs; grandson William Duiguid, 20 pounds; daughter, Ann Duiguid, my land and plantation whereon I now live excepting 30 a. above mentioned and all my slaves and accounts due me in Great Brittan and Virginia, my farm house and stock; rest of my grandchildren, Elizabeth Patteson, Isom Cole, Ann Duiguid, Martha Duiguid, and Mary Duiguid. Exrs.: my daughter, Ann Duiguid and Charles Patteson of Buckingham County. Wit.: John Poindexter, John Stratton, Caleb Crews.

Will of THOMAS WALTON, date 26 August 1771, Pro. 27 April 1772. Daughters, Elizabeth Miller and Patty Mosby; each of my sons, George, Thomas and Edward, 10 sh.; my son, Josiah Walton, 2 slaves; son, Robert Walton, 3 slaves; wife, Martha, one negro girl and all the rest of my estate; son, Josiah to have the upper moiety of land I now live on and the other moiety to my son, Robert; granddaughter, Lockey Walton. Exrs.: my wife, Martha Walton and my son, Thomas Walton. Wit.: George Cox, Henry Cox, Wm. Daniel.   Thomas Walton L.S.

Page 56: Will of SAMUEL BRIDGEWATER, dated 1st March 1772, Pro. 27 April 1772. Daughter, Susanna; sons, Thomas, William, Jesse, Samuel and Richard. I desire that John Jefferson do buy my land on North side of Little Groom's Quarter Creek at the north side at the rate of 15 sh. per acres and that my executors on his giving that sum make him a right to the same; son, Richard, land on North side of creek provided John Jefferson do not choose to buy; to daughter, Sarah, half of my personal estate; to daughter, Ann, the other half; the money arriving from my land mentioned for John Jefferson to be applied toward paying my debts. Exrs.:

friends, Alexander Trent and John Jefferson. Wit.: Wm. Hill, William Minter, Elizabeth Jefferson.
Samuel Bridgewater (X)

Page 57: Appraisal of estate of JOHNSON HODGES. Returned by: A. Davenport, Thos. Stegar, Chas. Scott. Approved 27 April 1772.

Page 58: Will of WILLIAM ELLIS, dated 14 November 1771, Pro. 28 May 1772. Mary Howard, 40 sh.; brother, Joseph Ellis; brother-in-law, John Clark; all my brothers and sisters equally to be divided the remainder of my estate. Ex.: Mathew Woodson. Wit.: Carroll Keen, Matthew Woodson.
William Ellis L.S.

Will of SARAH GUTTERY, dated 30 September 1771, Pro. 25 May 1772. Son, Bernard Guttery; son, William Coleman Guttery; daughter, Patty Guttery; grandson, Henry Guttery; grand-daughter, Lucy Elliott, daughter of my daughter, Philadelphia; granddaughter, Elizabeth Elliott; daughter, Orania Coleman; daughter, Susanna Lee; daughter, Grissell Meredith(?). Exrs.: my two sons, Bernard and William Coleman Guttery. Wit.: Gideon Edwards, Ann Glenn, Joseph Starkey.
Sarah Guttery (X)

Page 61: Appraisal of MARY MAXEY. Taken by Edward Maxey and Joseph Salle, Exrs. of last will of said deceased. Examined and approved 25 May 1772.

Page 62: Will of JACOB WINFREE, date 11 February 1772, Pro. 22 June 1772. Wife, Jane Winfree, one negro James, household goods and after her decease with one negro boy named Samson and the land whereon I now live to my son, Isaac; daughter, Ann Winfree, one negro girl Elanor; son, Charles, 25 pounds which my son, Jacob, justly owes; daughter, Sarah Robinson, 20 pounds which my son, Isaac, justly owes me. Exrs.: John Overton and Simon Gentry. Wit.: Jerimiah Barker, Charles Winfree, Jno. Overton.
Jacob Winfree

Page 63: Will of ELIZABETH PORTER, of King William Parish, dated 25 April 1772, Pro. 22 June 1772. My Isaac Porter; daughter, Mary Guerrant. Exrs.: my two sons, John and William Porter. Wit.: Hawkins Landrum, Shadrack Rosser, Sukey Landrum.

Page 64: Inventory and appraisal of estate of JOHN WOOLDRIDGE. By: Thos. Hall, William Street, John Dupuy. Court of 22 June 1772.

Page 65: Account of administration of Estate of ROBERT WALTON. By: Jas. Pleasants, Thos. Turpin, Jr. Court 27 July 1772.

Page 70: Will of RICE BENNETT, date August 5, 1770, Pro. 24 August 1772. Wife, Sarah; William Bennett, John Bennett; John to have 5 pounds to pay for his schooling more than his equal part. Exrs.: William Hambleton, John Jones, Sarah Bennett. Wit.: Robert Smith, William Hambleton, Joseph Jenkins, Ann Hambleton, (X).

Page 74: Appraisal of estate of EMERICH HUGHES given 12 August 1772 by: Charles Anderson, John Chambers, Moore Lumpkin. Court 24 August 1772.

Page 74: Inventory of estate of JOHN ARMISTEAD by William Armistead. Court 22 August 1772.

Page 75: Will of FRANCIS SPAULDING, date 20 January 1772, Pro.
24 August 1772. My dear wife, Elizabeth; my children,
John, Juda, Betsy, Polly, and Thomson. Ex.: Thomas Spaulding,
Jacob Spaulding, my wife, my son, John Spaulding. Wit.: John
Raine, Thos. Davenport, Jr., James Basham.

Francis Spaulding L.S.

Proved by John Raine and Thomas Davenport, Jr. Letters of Administration granted with securities: Moore Lumpkin and William
Angles, Jr., and Arehelaus Austin.

Will of BENJAMIN BEDFORD of Southam Parish, dated 31 May
1772, Pro. 24 August 1772. Wife, Susanna; two sons,
James Bedford and William Bedford; son, Stephen Bedford (under
21); daughter, Elizabeth Bedford; my desire is that my sons have
sufficient education and James to keep William if his estate will
afford it. Ex.: my brother, Thomas Bedford, Stephen Bedford,
Robert Smith, my wife, Susanna Bedford. Wit.: Wm. Smith, Jacob
Mosby, Wm. Ferguson.

Page 76: Will of MICAJAH MOSBY of Southam Parish, dated 15 June
1772, Pro. 28 September 1772. Wife, Moslin(?); my land
to be divided among my three children, Jesse, William and David
and David to have 300 acres where my house and plantation is and
the rest to be equally divided between Jesse and William; desire
that each of my daughters may have a horse and saddle of 10 pounds
value when they come of age. Ex.: Littlberry Mosby, Robert Smith,
my wife. Wit.: William Tucker, Sam'l. Mosby, Edward Linthicum.

Page 77: Inventory of estate of WILLIAM WEATHERFORD. By: William Hambleton, Joseph Jenkins and John Jones. Court of
28 September 1772.

Page 78: Will of DANIEL COLEMAN, dated 26 June 1772, Pro. 23 November 1772. Sons, Stephen and Spilsby Coleman, my land
in Pittsylvania County being 800 a.; son, James Coleman, 100 a.,
part of tract I live on to be laud off so as not to interfere
with my plantation; my sons, Daniel, Robert, Benjamin and William
80 pounds a piece; son, William, feather bed and furniture; son,
Joseph, feather bed and furniture; son, Benjamin, 1 horse; daughter, Lucy Barksdale; daughter, Elizabeth Allen; wife, Patience.
All my children, Stephen, James, Daniel, Spilsby, Robert, Benjamin, William and Joseph, Lucy Barksdale and Elizabeth Allen.
Exrs.: wife, Patience Coleman, Stephen Coleman, Robert Coleman,
Joseph Coleman and Benjamin Wilson. Wit.: Joseph Johns, Zachariah Hendrick, Patience Barksdale.

Signed: Daniel Coleman

Securities for administrators: Warren Walker and John Mayo.

Page __: Account of administration of estate of JOHN STEVENSON.
By: Jacob Mosby exr. Examined and ordered recorded
24 November 1772. By: Joseph Calland and Robert Smith.

Page __: Appraisal of estate of MICAJAH MOSBY. By: Robert
Bagby, William Stratton, William Tucker. Court
28 December 1772.

Page 84: Will of JOHN CHAFFIN, date 26 June 1767, Pro. 25 January 1773. My two sons, Christopher and Joshua; my two daughters Rachel Smith and Ruth Bradley. Ex.: son, Joseph Chaffin. Wit.: Henry Macon, John Slaughter, Robert Smith.

Appraisal of estate of ALEXANDER MOSS. Taken 3 day December 1772 by Robert Bagby, Jr., Jacob Mosby. Court 25 January 1773.

Page 86: Appraisal of estate of DANIEL COLEMAN. Taken 27 December 1772 by Moses Hudgens, William Davenport, Daniel Allen. Court 22 February 1773.

Will of JOSEPH HILL, Parish of Littleton, date 29 November 1772, Pro. 26 May 1777. Sons, Thomas and William, all my lands in Bedford County to be sold by me executor at any time and the money laid out in other lands for their use by an equal division as they come of age; son, Thomas; daughter, Elizabeth; daughter, Joyce; son, William; son, Thomas; son, Joseph, land where I now live after death of my wife; wife, Hannah, possession of all land whereon I now live with all the negroes and stock except the negroes above given away; my brother, John Hill, land in Halifax County on Cataba Creek. Exrs.: friends, Henry Macon and John Strange and Charles Barker and my wife, Hannah. Wit.: Joseph Starkey, John Burton, Stephen Woodson.
Joseph Hill L.S.

Page 91: Account of administration of estate of WILLIAM HUGHES with Simon Hughes administrator. Examined and ordered recorded Court 22 March 1773.

Page 92: Appraisal of estate of WILLIAM DUNGEE, JR. By: Matthew Sims, Zachary Hendrick, Benajah Thomson. Court 22 March 1773.

Appraisal of estate of JOHN CHAFFIN. Taken 22 March 1773 by: Robert Smith, John Slaughter, James Doss.

Appraisal of estate of JACOB AMMONETT. Given 18 November 1771 by: Charles Cottrell, John Chambers, Sam'l. Vawter. Court 22 March 1773.

Page 94: Appraisal of estate of ALEXANDER MOSS, deceased in Buckingham County. Taken by: William Phelp, Alex. Smith, Wm. Williams, John Brothers. Court 22 March 1773.

Page 94: Will of WILLIAM ALLEN BURTON, date 19 March 1767, Pro. 22 March 1773. Son, William Allen Burton, 250 acres in Cumberland County beginning where Walthall lives and....wife, plantation at the Dear Pons(?) during her life or marriage, after her death to my son, David Burton and my lot and house in Chesterfield County; Alex. Smith to divided among my five children, my estate when Walthall Burton comes of age and my two daughters to have 2 negroes a piece more than my sons viz: Mary and Sukey. Exrs.: my wife and Obey Smith. Wit.: John Price, William Parkinson, Philip Yates Jobson.

Page 95: Appraisal of estate of DAVID LE SEUER. By: Rolfe Eldridge, William Salle, Francis Mosby. Made 22 April 1773, Court 26 April 1773.

Page 96: Appraisal of estate of RICE BENNETT. By: Charles Barker, Samuel Melton, John Burton. Given 26 March 1773, Appr. 26 April 1773.

Page 98: Account of administration of estate of JOHN MERRYMAN.
          By: Samuel Povall, John Jefferson. Taken 22 March
1773, Court 26 April 1773.

Page 99: Inv. and Appraisal of Estate of ELIZABETH PORTER. By:
          Abraham Sandifer, ...Martin, Matt Bingley. Court
26 April 1772.

Page 100: Will of DAVID SISER, date 4 September 1771, Pro.
           26 April 1773. Wife, Mary; Children, Bartlet, John,
David, Thomas, Henderson, Mary and Sarah. Ex.: son, John and my
wife, Mary. Wit.: Jedethan Carter, Jesse Carter, Wm. Pride.

Page 101: Appraisal of estate of SAMUEL WRIGHT. Given 20 Feb-
           ruary 1773 by: Charles Anderson, Saymore Scott, John
Woodson. Court 26 April 1773.

           Inventory of estate of BENJAMIN BEDFORD.

Page 102: Account of Sales of Estate of BENJAMIN BEDFORD.
           April 2, 1773; 25 May 1773.

           Appraisal of Estate of DAVID SIZER. By: Henry Bagby,
           Jacob Mayo, David Lemay. 24 May 1773.

Page 103: Will of JOHN RADFORD of Southam Parish, dated 29 July
           1772, Pro. 28 June 1773. Son, Richard, land whereon
I now live; grandson, Richard Epperson, 125 acres of land whereon
he now lives; my daughter, Susana Epperson to have liberty of
living on said land during her life; grandson, John Epperson; my
wife, the rest of my estate during her life and after her death
to be equally divided between my children (did not name them).
Ex.: my beloved wife and sons, George and Richard Radford.
Wit.: Edward Parrott, William Blackburn (X), James Blackburn.
                              Signed: John Radford

Page 194: Will of ROBERT MC LAURINE of Southam Parish, dated
           May 7, 1771, Pro. 26 July 1773. Wife, Elizabeth,
200 a. land being part of land I bought of Poindexter Mosby to
include the plantation now on the said land together with four
negroes; son, William, 2 slaves when he reaches age of 21; daughter, Katherine, 2 slaves when she reaches age of 18; daughter,
Elizabeth, 3 negros when she reaches age of 18; my two sons,
James and William, the rest of my land purchased of Poindexter
Mosby and George Chambers being 433 a. Exrs.: my wife, Elizabeth and George Carrington, Jr., Joseph Calland. Wit.: Jesse
Carter, Junr., M. Carrington, L. Mosby, Junr.
                              Signed: Robert McLaurine

Page 194: Inventory of estate of WILLIAM ALLEN BURTON. By:
           Mary Burton. Court 26 July 1773.

Page 107: Will of JAMES TAYLOR of Southam Parish, dated
           January 23, 1772, Pro. 23 August 1773. To my wife....
Elizabeth, use of my land and plantation during her widowhood or
at least until my son James Taylor comes to age of 21 then for
him to possess where his grandmother Aviss Taylor now lives; all
that tract to be equally divided between James Taylor and Fargis-
son Taylor, his brother; son, Clement Taylor, land and plantation
where Duncan Robertson now lives; son, John Taylor, 200 a.; son,
Hughes Taylor; daughter, Martha Taylor, land which her grandfather John Taylor did bequeath to her in his last will to be
sold at discretion of my executors, the money to be divided

between my three youngest sons and youngest daughter, viz: Hughes
Taylor, Samuel Taylor, William Taylor and Elizabeth Taylor, Clement
Taylor having but a small parcel of land I desire that he should
have part of said estate for his 40 a. of land to be made up as
much as his other three youngest brothers and sister's legacies
amount to. Exrs.: my wife, Elizabeth Taylor and her father,
John Hughes and my friend, William Fleming. Wit.: William Taylor, Robert Taylor, Betty Taylor.   James Taylor

Page 108: Appraisal of estate of JOSEPH HILL. Maurice Langhorne,
           Daniel Allen, Mark Andrews. Court 23 August 1773.

Page 110: Appraisal of estate of NATHAN ROBINSON. Ben Wilson,
           Robert Brown, Jno. Jefferson. Court 23 August 1773.

Page 110: Will of THOMAS HILL, dated 6 October 1770, Pro. 25 Oct-
           ober 1773. Son, John Hill, 100 a.; son, Dennett Hill;
daughter, Sarah; daughter, Mary; sons, Thomas, William, Joseph
and James and my daughter, Ann; wife, Barchenay(?). Ex.: son,
Dennett Hill. Wit.: John Starkey, Joseph Starkey, John Spearman.
                                             Thomas Hill (X)

Page 112: Will of STEPHEN FORSEE, date 8 November 1772, Pro.
           22 November 1773. Son, Stephen Forsee, 1100 a.; son,
John Forsee, land that joins Peter Harris, Judith Bingley; son,
Francis Forsee; my wife, plantation where I now live also slaves
during her life; my children, Charles, William and Elizabeth, to
get slaves after their mother's death; my five daughters and my
2 sons, Charles and William; daughter, Judith Price; daughter,
Ann Martin; land I have in Buckingham County on Hugh Green's
Creek may be sold; my four daughters, Mary Ann Mari(?), Ann
Martin, Jane Briant and Judith Price. Exrs.: sons, Stephen and
Francis Forsee. Wit.: Abraham Sandefer, George Stovall Smith,
Dudley Street.

Page 114: Appraisal and inventory of estate of JOHN CARTER.
           Jas. Gilliam, Jr., Wm. Dillon, Sr., Jno. Creasy.
Court 22 November 1773.

Page 115: Will of ANN MAYO, dated 22 January 1769. Son, Joseph
           Mayo; grandson, Daniel Mayo; granddaughter, Mary Macon;
granddaughter, Ann Macon; daughter-in-law, Ann Carrington; grandson, William Mayo, son of John Mayo, choice of lots in two of
New Glasgow; grandson, John Mayo, lot in town of New Glasgow;
son, John Mayo, all my land in Cumberland County, also slaves;
granddaughter, Mary Ann Mayo. Exr.: son, John Mayo. Wit.:
Thomas Ballow, John Hughes, John .... (X), Richard Cardwell.
                                    Signed: Ann Mayo

Codicil to will of ANN MAYO, 27 January 1770, Pro. 27 December
1773. Wit.: Joseph Harris, Benjamin Harris, John Hughes (X).
All the personal estate which I declare that I have I declare
that I have a right to dispose of to my grandchildren whether
before given or not may be for and go equally among the children
of John Mayo except what I have given to Mary Ann Mayo which I
desire may be for her and it is further my desire that the hole
that I have given to any person and whatever is on the plantation
at time of my death may stay and be on the plantation for use and
benefit of my estate till 22nd February which shall be after the
date of my death then if anyone interrupt my executors, then they
shall claim no benefit and all go to my son, John.

Page 116: Appraisal of estate of ANTHONY NORTH. Alex. Guttery,

Benjah Thomson, Richard Allen. Court 24 January 1774.

Page 117: Appraisal of estate of WILLIAM BASKETT, deceased,
          24 November 1773. Joseph Price, John Price, John
Nuston. Court 24 January 1774 recorded.

Page 119: Appraisal of estate of DUNCAN BUCHANAN. Francis M.
          Crow, Robt. Biscoe, Jos. Harris. Court 28 February
1774.

Page 120: Will of ISAAC DUFFEE of Littleton Parish, date 2 Jan-
          uary 1774, Pro. 28 February 1774. Son, Edmon, 100 a.
of land together with the plantation I purchased of William Owens
as soon as he is 21; lend to my wife, Mary Duffee residue of my
estate during her widowhood and at her death to my son, Isaac
Duffee the plantation with 150 a. of land where I now live. If
either of my sons dies before he arrives to age of 21, the other
to have his land and at death of my wife, my will is that all my
estate to be equally divided between all my children to-wit:
Mary, Edmon, Elisabeth, Henry, Polly, Salley, Kessia and Isaac
except Mary to have 5 pounds less that the rest as I have given
her that quantity before. Ex.: my wife and Warren Walker. Wit.:
William Walker, Benjamin Walker.   Isaac Duffee (X)

Page 122: Inventory of estate of DRURY BAUGHTWRIGHT, deceased.
          Take February 18, 1774. Edmond Logwood. Court
28 February 1774.

Page 122: Account of administration of estate of CHARLES HOLLAND.
          By: John Scott adm. taken May 17, 1771. Court
24 March 1774.

Page 123: In obedience to order of court date 25 January 1772,
          we the subscribers have settled the above account on
examination of George Carrington, Jr. one of the executors of
John Scott, deceased, on each and find balance as above stated
to bear interest from 17 May 1771 until paid given under our hand
12 March 1774. L. Mosby, Chas. Scott. Account of administration
of estate of Charles Holland examined and ordered recorded
24 March 1774.

Page 123: Inventory of estate of JOHN REDFORD taken March 2,
          1773. George Radford, Richard Radford. Court
28 March 1774.

Page 124: Appraisal of estate of ROBERT DINWIDDIE. Court
          28 March 1774.

Page 124: Will of WADE NETHERLAND, dated November 12, 1773, Pro.
          29 April 1774. Daughter, Frances Netherland, all the
negroes and their increase left by my father and now in possession
of my sister, Frances Macon, wife of Henry Macon; if she dies
without issue, negros to be equally divided between five children
of my sister, Mary, wife of Tucker Woodson, viz: Wade Woodson,
Sarah Woodson; Frances Netherland, negro; all my lands; my wife,
Ann Netherland, negro with all my moveable estate. Ex.: wife,
Ann Netherland with Henry Macon and Jacob Michaux. Wit.: Julius
Allen, James Price.

Page 125: Estate of RICE BENNETT in account with Thomas Linc-
          thieum, account of administration. Maurice Langhorne,
Adcock Hobson, Thomas Nash. Ex. and rec. 25 April 1774.

Page 127: Inventory and appraisal of estate of ISAAC DUFFEE,
           deceased. Appraised and sworn to Matthew Nelson,
Valentine Callas(?), John Holeman. Warren Walker, exr., Mary
Duffee (X). Rec. court May 23, 1774.

Page 128: Appraisal of estate of JAS. MEREDITH and account of
           administration. Wit.: Jon Fleming, late att. at law,
deceased. Geo. Carrington, L. Mosby.

Page 131: Will of DANIEL WILMORE, date November 2, 1773. My
           land of John Johns and Robert Johns, sons of my niece,
Jane Johns; niece, Elisabeth Howl, 5 pounds; niece, Jane Johns
and her ch. Ex.: John Hughes and William Johns, eldest son of
my niece, John Johns. Wit.: Wm. Fleming, Bennett Goode.

Page 132: Will of JACOB MICHAUX, dated June 1, 1774, Pro. 27 June
           1774. Wife, Sally Michaux; three daughters, Sally,
Judith and Lucy; my others daughter; son, Jacob, my ferry and
land from Paul Michaux line to that of Joseph Michaux; I leave
John Hughs to management of his mother till he comes to age of 21.
Ex.: John Michaux, Abraham Venable, William Smith, Robert Smith.
Wit.: Simion Harris, James Bryden, Hugh French, James Wilkenson.
                              Signed: Jacob Michaux

Page 135: Account of estate of RICE BENNETT. Administration by
           Thomas Linthicum and his wife, Sarah executrix. By:
Adcock Hobson, Thomas Nash, Frederick Hobson. Court 25 July 1774.

Page 137: Estate of JAMES HARRIS in account with executor of
           said estate. Ex. and ordered recorded 25 July 1774.
Thomas Turpin, Jr., Ant. Martin, Wm. Fleming.

Page 137: Will of JOHN HUGHES, date 16 April 1774, Pro. 22 Aug-
           ust 1774. Wife, Judith; son, John Hughes; in case
Jacob Michaux does not live to see my son, John, come of age, I
desire that he leave my son to care of any person he thinks for
that purpose. Exrs.: wife, Judith, John Woodson, Jacob Michaux.
Wit.: Peter Stone, John K. Read, Jere. Rust.
                              John Hughes

Page 139: Appraisal of estate of MICAJAH MOSBY. August 22, 1774
           by: Francis ME Crow(?), Jno. Barnes, John Phelps,
Junr. Court 22 August 1774.

           Appraisal of Estate of JESSE OSLIN, deceased. By:
           Edmund Price, Martin Richardson, James Austin. Court
August 22, 1774.

Page 140: Appraisal of Estate of MARY MAYO, deceased. Returned
           by: James Drake, George Owen, Edmond Toney. Court
11 July 1773.

           A further appraisal of estate of MARY MAYO, July 22,
           1773 by: George Owen, Edmond Toney, James Drake, Wm.
Taylor.

           A further appraisal February 17, 1774. Wm. Taylor,
           Edmond Toney, Sr., James Drake.

Page 141: Appraisal and inventory of MARY MAYO ordered recorded
           26 September 1774.

Page 141: Inventory of estate of DANIEL WILMORE'S estate. Exhibited and ordered recorded 26 September 1774.

Page 141:   Will of RICHARD HARRIS, dated 17 June 1774, Pro. 26
            September 1774. All my estate to be equally divided
between my brother and sisters with this proviso only that one
negro man named Dick and now in service of Mr. Ryland Randolph
of Henrico County shall continue to be joint property of all my
brothers and sisters aforesaid and be anually hired to some as
discreet person and the profits of his labour be equally divided
as above until my youngest brother shall arrive to the full age
of 21 and then the said negro to be sold in the family only that
is to any of my brothers and sisters that shall be the highest
bidder and maintain him for life on the easiest terms in case he
should be past his labour. I appoint the Rev. Christopher Mac
Rae of Cumberland County sole executor of this my last will and
testament. Wit.: Ben Moseley, Thomas H. Drew, William Harris.

Page 145:   Will of BENJAMIN MOSBY of Southam Parish, dated 8 Day
            March 1771, Pro. 26 September 1774. Son, Littleberry
Mosby, all my land in Buckingham County, also all my land called
the Court House land and the land I bought of Philip Poindexter,
also 10 slaves, my waggon and 4 horses also every kind of furniture and other thing in and belonging to my house called the new
House, also my 4 large oxen and ox cart and my silver watch; to
my loving wife, Mary, during her natural life or widowhood, use
of my slaves, also 3 back rooms in the house called the ordinary
and a small house called her store, a small house called the
dairy, the building added to my kitchen and my small plank floored
stable; I also lend unto my wife the use of the following things,
three feather beds and furniture, one bed called the overseer's,
three tables and a dozen leather chairs and ½ dozen chairs, etc.;
to son, Poindexter Mosby, all lands bought of Woodson and Barksdale which I possesed him with, and the land I lately recovered
of James Daniels and other adjoining the land of Maurice Langhorne and others; to my son, Poindexter, all the slaves he is now
possessed of by virtue of a gift; to my daughter, Mary Ann Netherland, slaves and other estate she is now possessed with; to my
daughter, Theodocia Carrington, negroes I possessed her with and
all my negroes, also furniture I have possessed her with; to my
granddaughter, Mary Netherland, a negro woman; to my granddaughter, Elizabeth Netherland, negro; if any granddaughter die without issue, said negro to her father, John Netherland; my will is
that my son, Littleberry and Poindexter divide my wearing apparel
after giving Seth Birton a full suit of my common clothes; to my
son, Littleberry, all my plantation utensils except such as I
have lent to his mother, also all the money I may die possessed
of and all my outstanding debts he paying all the debts I may owe.
All the estate I have not given to be equally divided among my
children, Littleberry, Poindexter, Mary, Ann, and Theodocia,
share and share alike. I desire my estate not to be appraised
and that if any dispute arises then my friends, George Carrington,
Thompson Swann, John Woodson and William Smith do settle the same.
Exrs.: my sons, Littleberry Mosby and Poindexter Mosby and son-
in-law, John Netherland and Joseph Carrington. Wit.: Jno. Overton, Thompson Swann.   Benj. Mosby L.S.

Page 149:   Will of SAMUEL ALLEN of Littleton Parish, date Jan-
            uary 4, 1774, Pro. 26 September 1774. To my son,
Archer Allen, all my land lying on Cub Creek in Charlotte County
containing 900 a. more or less whereon his people are now settled;
to said son, negro Stephen; to son, Samuel Allen, all the land
and plantation whereon I now live, 625 a. after the death of my
beloved wife, Martha; if he should die without issue, then said

land to be sold and the money divided equally between all my
children; to daughter, Mary, 2 negroes Benn and Cloe provided she
will keep same in her own possession but not to be sold or hired
out and after her death to be divided among her children. And
if she does not have any negroes to return to my estate and be
equally divided with rest of my estate; my desire is that my said
daughter, Mary, have full use of one small room in my house where
shed opens onto the chamber where I usually lodge and that she
freely possess the same as long as she lives unmarried and if she
marries during her natural life I likewise give her one feather
bed and furniture; to daughter, Elizabeth Jefferson; to daughter,
Judah Massey; to daughter, Pattyfield Daniel; to daughter,
Obedience Towns; to daughter, Frances; to daughter, Ann; if son
Fueld live longer that his mother, then my son-in-law, William
Daniel take him home and take care of him as long as he lives
and in consideration thereof I give said William Daniel one
negro winch. Exrs.: my two sons, Archer and Samuel Allen and
my son-in-law, William Daniel. Wit.: Stephen Woodson, Lucy
Woodson, George Parker, Wm. Town.

Page 152: Will of GEORGE WRIGHT of Littleton Parish, dated
            July 8, 1774, Pro. 26 September 1774. My loving
friend, Elizabeth Armstrong during her life, one negro man named
Joe and negro Wason Cole and negro girl Hannah, also an equal
part with my children of my personal estate, also 1 feather bed
and furniture, also lend her for life 300 a. of land joining
Samuel Williams and Alexander Trent to be laid off by my executors and it is also my will that she may have a good dwelling
house 16 X 24 ft., a kitchen and all other necessary houses and
gardens built on said land and that she have possession of the
houses where I now live for the term of 5 years after my decease
and after her decease it is my will that the land and all the
other estate I have lent be sold and equally divided amongst all
my children hereafter named, Henry Wright, George Wright, William
Wright, Archibald Wright, Thomas Wright, Mary Wright, Gabriel
Wright, Sarah Wright; I leave a slave to each of children, the
remaining part of my land to be divided among my sons, and also
negroes to be divided; the remaining personal estate due me
(debts) to be collected and my part of the mill to be equally
divided among my children. Exrs.: my two brothers, Thomas
Wright and Griffin Wright and my two sons, George and William
Wright. Wit.: John Lee, Griffin Wright, Saymore Scott, William
Shepard.

Page 154: Will of JAMES GILLIAM of Littleton Parish, dated
            28 October 1774, Pro. 24 October 1774. Son, James,
and if he dies without heirs, land to be divided among rest of
my children; I desire a dividing line to be drawn from a marked
white oak near where my path leaves Daniel's road to go a little
above my plantation patch to Woodson line and all that part that
will lie on that side the line where my dwelling house stands I
land to my wife. I give the same to my grandson, Charles Manning
Gilliam at death of my said wife; to grandson, Robert Gilliam,
remainder of the tract of land I now live on; I desire son, James
have use of land during minority of my said grandson only that he
shall not have liberty to cut down or clean any on the upper side
of commons branch; son-in-law, Joseph Taylor; son-in-law, Martin
King and his wife; grandson, Gilliam King; daughter, Sally
Gilliam; granddaughter, Sarah Taylor. I desire my daughter,
Sally to live with my wife as long as my said daughter shall be
single. Exr.: son, James Gilliam, son-in-law, Joseph Taylor.
Wit.: G. Carrington, Jr., Lucy Manning, John Creasy.
                    Signed: James Gilliam (X)

Page 167: Will of WILLIAM ARNOLD, date 16 September 1774, Pro.
            28 November 1774. Son, Moses Arnold, 200 a. being
land and plantation whereon he now lives; son, Thomas Arnold,
100 a. being land and plantation whereon he now lives; son, Moses,
one large pewter dish and one large pewter bason; wife, Elizabeth,
use of all my estate real and personal during her natrual life and
after her death my estate to be divided among all my children.
Exrs.: three sons, Moses, John and Thomas Arnold. Wit.: Adcock
Hobson, Benjamin Sims, John Bowler.

Page 158: Will of JUDITH COX, date 27 June 1774, Pro. 28 Novem-
            ber 1774. Whole estate to my son, Josiah Cox. Ex.:
son, Josiah Cox. Wit.: Frederick Hatcher, William Gray.

Page 159: Will of JEREMIAH RUST, date 12 October 1774, Pro.
            28 November 1774. To Frances Mims Stoner, 1 negro
girl; my wife Frances Rust, rest of my estate. Ex.: trusty
friend, Benj. Stoner and my wife Frances Rust. Wit.: Vincent
Harland, William Spears, Robert Davies (X).

Page 159: Inventory of estate of WADE NETHERLAND. By: James
            Bagby, Anthony Minter, Edward Cox. 2 May 1774. Court
29 November 1774.

Page 162: Appraisal of estate of SETH BURTON. Returned 23 Dec-
            ember 1774 by: Fred'l. Hatcher, Adcock Hobson,
Hezekiah Colquit. Court 26 December 1774.

Page 163: Will of THOMAS WILLBOURN, date 10 November 1774, Pro.
            26 December 1774. Wife, Christian, all my estate
during her natural life or as long as she remains my widow, in
case of marriage then my land to be equally divided between my
two sons, Robert and Thompson Wilbourn and the remaining part to
be divided between her and my children. Exrs.: Littleberry
Mosby, Joseph Carrington. Wit.: Jacob Mosby, Wm. Smith, William
Willbourn.

Page 164: Appraisal of the estate of WILLIAM ARNOLD by: William
            Davenport, Henry Davenport, David Davenport. 23 Jan-
uary 1775, Court 23 January 1775.

Page 164: Will of THOMAS LOCKETT, date 8 September 1770, Pro.
            23 January 1775. Son, Stephen, my land in Prince
Edward county on South side of Harrises creek; son, Abner Lockett,
land where I now live; son, Jacob, all my land on Nuttree branch
in Chesterfield when he comes to age of 21; daughter, Martha
Bass, all my land on North side of Harrises creek from the cross
line of my son Stephen to upper line; daughter, Lucey Stone, land
on South side of North Cork of Falling Creek and also 20 a. of
the North side; daughter, Elizabeth Lockett; daughter, Mary Gipson; wife, Judith Lockett, land in Prince Edward County not
already willed away to be sold and the money equally divided
among all my children except James. All the rest to be divided
among all my children, James, Stephen, David, Abner, Jacob
Lockett and Martha Bass, Lucey Stone, Mary Gipson and Elizabeth
Lockett. Exrs.: sons, Stephen and Abner Lockett and Arthur
Moseley. Wit.: Gideon Lockett, John Gipson, Robt. Haskins.
                                        Thomas Lockett L.S.

Page 167: Appraisal of the estate of JUDITH COX, date February 4,
            1775. By: Josiah Thomson, Henry Cox, William Daniel.

Page 167: Will of ANDREW EDWARDS, date April 7, 1774, Pro.

58

27 February 1775. To wife, Elizabeth, I lend my
plantation whereon I now live and the liberty to clear what
ground joining the plantation as she shall think proper; son,
William, plantation where he now lives; my executors to pay my
son William 2 shillings 6 pence after my wife's death and my son,
William's death then I give all my land to my son, Andrew Edwards
with every other part or kind of estate whatsoever except what I
shall hereafter mention; my two daughters, Moutry Edwards and
Patsy Edwards; my two daughters, Catherine Walker and Elizabeth
Walker, 2 shillings and 6 pence. Ex.: Francis Flipping, Thomas
Walton. Wit.: William Bernard, Mary Bernard, Elizabeth Bernard.
                                        Andrew Edwards

Page 169: Appraisal of the estate of RICHARD CLARK. By: Simon
          Gentry, Christopher Robinson, Richd. Richardson, Edwd.
Robertson. Court 27 February 1775.

Page 169: The will of JOHN JAMES DUPUY, of King William and
          Cumberland Counties, date 9 February 1775, Pro. 27
February 1775. To son, Bartholomew Dupuy, 400 a. in Amelia
County being land whereon he now lives; granddaughter, Susanna
Dupuy, daughter of my son, Bartholomew; son, John Dupuy, 200 a.
of land I purchased of John Durham, also 200 a. part of tract I
now dwell on; son, James Dupuy, remainder of tract whereon I now
live, also land I bought of my brother, Peter Dupuy; daughter,
Olimpt(?) Trabue, 200 a.; grandson, Benjamin Hatcher, 100 a. in
Amelia County; daughter, Martha Foster, 380 a. in Amelia County;
daughter, Mary Hatcher; daughter, Elizabeth Dupuy, 20 a.; daugh-
ter, Martha Foster, 190 a. in Amelia County, grandson, George
Foster; granddaughter, Susanna Foster, 30 pounds; grandson, John
Lockett, son of my daughter, Susanna Lockett 200 a. of land which
his father, James Lockett, has in his possession; grandsons,
James, Joel and Brattain Lockett, sons of my daughter, Susanna
Lockett, 60 pounds when they arrive to age of 21; granddaughter,
Susanna Trabue; granddaughter, Susanna Hatcher; granddaughter,
Mary Foster; my seven children. Exrs.: two sons, Bartholomew
Dupuy and James Dupuy and son-in-law, Benj. Hatcher. Wit.: Wm.
Street, James Bryant, Jun., Benjamin Watkins.

Page 173: Appraisal of estate of JOHN HUGHES by: Harry Bagby,
          Jas. Bagby and Bennett Goode. Court 27 February 1775.

Page 173: Will of THOMAS DAVENPORT, date December 16, 1773, Pro.
          27 March 1775. Son, James Davenport; son, Thomas
Davenport; son, Henry Davenport; son, William Davenport; daughter
Drucilla Glenn; grandson, Stephen Davenport, son of Stephen;
granddaughter, Molly Davenport, daughter of Stephen. Ex.: Gideon Glenn. Wit.: Joseph Jenkins, James Coleman Glen, Lucy Jenkins (X).   Thomas Davenport (X)

Page 176: Appraisal of estate of JAMES GILLIAM. By: Drury
          Woodson, Hezekiah Davidson, Sam'l. Robinson. Decem-
ber 12, 1774, Court 24 April 1775.

Page 177: Will of WILLIAM DANIEL, date 8 March 1771, Pro. 24
          April 1775. Son, William, 200 a. I purchased of my
brother, James Daniel, lying in this county on Soke Arse Creek,
joining land of Alex Trent, Bradley and Thomas Holland; to son,
William, one boy; to daughter, Judith, negro girl Silva; to
daughter, Elizabeth, negro boy now in possession of her and her
husband John Fuqua; to daughter, Sarah, negro girl; to daughter,
Mary, negro girl, Judah now in possession of said daughter and
her husband, John Nelson; my son, William Pride, negro boy; son,

Hezekiah; son, John (under 21); daughter, Rhoda; wife, Elizabeth; son, Benjamin. Exrs.: sons, William, Benjamin, William Price, Hezekiah and John. Wit.: Joseph Starkey, ... Guthrey(?).

William Daniel

Page 180: Will of RICHARD EPPERSON of Southam Parish, dated 13 November 1774, Pro. April 24, 1775. My sister-in-law, Biddy Maxey; Jamima Sally, my sister-in-law, wife of Joseph Sallie, use of my estate I had before my contract marriage with my deceased wife, Keziah; to Susannah Epperson, my mother. Ex.: Joseph Sallie, George Radford. Wit.: Edward Toms, Nathaniel Maxey (X).

Richd. Epperson (X)

Page 181: Will of LEANDER HUGHES of Littleton Parish, dated 24 March 1775, Pro. 28 June 1775. Son, Powell (or Povall) Hughes, upper half of tract of land whereon I now live; son, Stephen Hughes, the other half; son, John Hughes; my sons, Powell Hughes, Archelaus Hughes and Stephen Hughes; grandson, John Watkins; land in Charles County to be sold. Exrs.: Powell Hughes, Archelaus Hughes. Wit.: Hannah Saunders, Deanche(?) Browdert (X).

Leander Hughes (X)

Page 182: Will of JESSE SCRUGGS, date 29 December 1774, Pro. 24 July 1775. Loving wife, Rebeccah, my hole estate. Ex.: wife, Rebeccah Scruggs and my father, Robert Scruggs. Wit.: Tabitha Scruggs (X), Simon Hughes, John Flippen.

Jesse Scruggs L.S.

Page 183: Will of MARK ANDREWS of Littleton Parish, dated 9 November 1774, Pro. 24 July 1775. My three sons, John, Thomas, and Garnett Andrews, the land and plantation I have in Prince Edward County; my two sons, William and Wiatt, land and plantation whereon I now live; my son, Jesse; daughter, Mary Griffin; my four sons, William, Thomas, Garnett and Wiatt; daughter, Susanna Andrews; daughter, Ann Andrews; my 8 children, John, William, Thomas, Garnett, Wiatt, Hannah, Susannah and Ann. Exrs.: two sons, John and William Andrews. Wit.: James Doss, John Doss.

Mark Andrews L.S.

Page 184: Will of JOSEPH JONS (JOHNS), Southam Parish, dated 13 January 1775, Pro. 24 July 1775. Wife, Jane Johns, land whereon I now live during her natural life or widowhood and then to be divided between my two oldest sons, William and Joseph Jons; wife, my whole estate and at her death to be divided between my children, William Jons, Judy Farriss, and Joseph Jons and John Jons and Marthy Jons, and Robert Jons and Jane Jons. Es.: wife, Jane Jons and son, William Jons. Wit.: James Bresham, Bennett Goode.

Joseph Jons (X)

When this will was proved the court records has that it was Joseph Johns and proved by his wife, Jane Johns, extrx.

Page 185: Will of WILLIAM PARKER of King William Parish, dated 29 January 1775, Pro. 28 August 1775. Wife, Magdalene Parker; son, Stephen, land whereon I now live; son, Thomas, land on Jones Creek; son, Chastain Parker; son, William Parker; son, Peter Parker; my five sons. Ex.: my wife and brother, John Parker. Wit.: Josiah Hatcher, Peter Sublet, Jr., William Benton.

Signed: Wm. Parker L.S.

Page 185: Inventory of estate of SAMUEL ALLEN. By: Archer Allen, Wm. Daniel, Sam'l. Allen. Court 28 August 1775.

Page 187: Appraisal of estate of EDWARD MOSBY, 28 August 1775.
          Settlement of accounts of Edward Mosby made by John
Peter Bondurant and Patty, his wife and Jesse Miller, admrs. of
said estate.

Page 188: Will of PETER HARRIS of King William Parish, date
          15 February 1771, Pro. 28 August 1775. Son, Henry
Harris, land on Dutoy's branch after death of my wife, Elizabeth
Harris whereon I now live; son, John Harris; daughter, Susannah;
daughter, Eleanor and her husband William Guttery (Guthrey?);
granddaughter, Mary Guttery, daughter of Eleanor; grandson, Peter
Guttery; daughter, Elizabeth's children (was lately wife of Peter
Walker); daughter, Sarah; daughter, Ann Harris; granddaughter,
Ann, daughter of my daughter, Susannah; daughter, Mary. Exrs.:
my wife, Elizabeth Harris and Charles Clarke. Wit.: Daniel
Guerrant, Mary Guerrant (X), Peter Depp, Chas. Clarke.

Page 193: JOHN COOK, dated 15 April 1775, Pro. 25 September 1775.
          All my land in Buckingham that is in dispute with
Benjamin Arnold and land whereon I now live, etc., to my wife,
Mary, during her life or widowhood and after her decease to be
equally divided between my son, Stephen Cook, Mary, Noell, and
Frances Cook, Aggy Chambers, Sarah Edwards, Elizabeth Hooper,
James Cook, Agathy Bostick, Ann Coleman. Exrs.: George Hooper
and my son, Stephen Cook. Wit.: John Raine, Henry Walker.
                              Signed: John Cook (X)

Page 194: Will of THOMAS DAVENPORT of Littleton Parish, date
          29 September 1774, Pro. 25 September 1775. Son, James;
son, Thomas; son, Henry; son, Julius, land and plantation; son,
William; grandson, William Davenport, son of Stephen, deceased;
daughter, Drucilla Glenn, negro woman in possession of Gideon
Glenn; daughter, Drucilla Glenn and her husband; the several
children of my daughter, Drucilla Glenn; grandson, Stephen Davenport, son of my son Stephen, deceased; granddaughter, Molly
Davenport; my sons, Thomas, Henry, William and my daughter,
Drucilla Glenn. Exrs.: Thomas Davenport, Henry Davenport,
William Davenport and Gideon Glenn. Wit.: Davis Davenport,
and Shean(?) Cook.

Page 196: Account of administration of estate of JOHN SCOTT
          returned by George Carrington, Jr. Examined by: L.
Mosby, Chas. Scott. 30 June 1775, Court 23 October 1775.

Page 197: Inventory of estate of WILLIAM PARKER. By: Magdalene
          Parker, John Parker, Sr., exrs. October 18, 1775,
Court 23 October 1775.

Page 198: Inventory of estate of JONAS MEADOR, deceased. By:
          Wm. Saunderson, Senr., Sam'l. Atkinson, Martin Wilker-
son (X). Court 23 October 1775.

Page 199: Inventory and Appraisal of estate of GEORGE WRIGHT.
          By: John Holman, Miller Woodson and John Woodson.
Court 27 November 1775.

Page 202: Appraisal of estate of MARK ANDREWS, deceased. By:
          Henry Macon, Robert Smith, John Noell. Court 27 Jan-
uary 1776.

Page 203: Will of DAVID WINNIFORD of Southam Parish, dated
          January 2, 1771, Pro. 22 January 1776. Grandson,
George Cunningham (under age); grandsons, David Winniford and

61

Charles Winniford; my grandson, David Winniford; my neighbor,
Jacob McGehee to take the negro Matt, Ned and Jammy into his
possession and care and to keep them together with their increase
of the said Matt until my grandchildren shall have a right to
demand them respectively and that the said Jacob pay unto whomso-
ever shall have right to demans Matt such hire as he shall think
sufficient for her service after satisfying himself for clothing
and maintaining her and her children; unto Isham Bradley and
William Bradley one feather bed and furniture as belongs to it
at time of my decease, etc.; grandson, George Cunningham; grandsons, David and Charles and George. Ex.: Jacob McGehee. Wit.:
Thomson Swann, Catherine Swann, Jenett Swann.

David Winniford (X)

Page 205: Will of JOHN HICKS, dated 7 May 1775, Pro. 22 January
1776. Daughter, Elizabeth Rawling; lend to my wife,
Mary during her life, the land and plantation whereon I now live
and all the rest of my estate; after her death, land, etc. to be
sold and the money to be equally divided between Henry Hicks,
John Hicks and Mary Hicks and Nathaniel Hicks and Clayborn Hicks
and Susanna Hicks and Jesse Hicks. Exrs.: Thomas Wilkinson and
my wife, Mary Hicks. Wit.: Martin Allen, John Armistead,
William Armistead.

Page 205: Will of JOHN JONES, dated May 4, 1775, Pro. 22 January
1776. Wife, Ann Jones, all my estate, if she marry,
the estate to be equally divided between my wife and my children,
Guinivere(?), Susanna, Samuel and Mary, son, William Jones; I
desire my younger children to be educated at the discretion of my
executors. Exrs.: friend, William Jones of Bedford County,
Evan Ragland, John Ragland, his son, both of Halifax County.
Wit.: C. H. Harrison, Sally Wood, Elizabeth Farlines.

John Jones (X)

Page 207: Appraisal of estate of JOSEPH JOHNS, deceased. By:
Henry Bagby, Bartlet Siser(?), William Bates. Court
22 January 1776.

Page 206: Inventory of estate of WILLIAM DANIEL, deceased.
Court 22 January 1776.

Page 207: Appraisal of estate of ANDREW EDWARDS. By: Martin
Richardson (X), John Johnson(?), William Powell or
Povall.

Page 208: Will of EDWARD MATHIAS, dated September 13, 1775, Pro.
22 January 1776. Wife, Elizabeth Mathias; daughter,
Nancy Mathias; son, Ussery Mathias. Exrs.: wife, Elizabeth and
Benj. Wilson. Wit.: Frances Glen, Tabitha Barnes (X), Benjamin
Allen.

Appraisal of estate of RICHARD HARRIS. By: Charles
Barker, Thos. Guttrey, Alex. Guthrey. Court 26 January 1776.

Page 209: Appraisal of estate of PETER HARRIS in obedience to
court order of 25 September 1775. By: James Bryant,
Sam'l. Flourney, Arthur Mosely. Dated 20 October 1775. Court
21 February 1776.

Page 210: Will of CATHERINE MC LAURINE of Southam Parish, dated
8 September 1775, Pro. 26 February 1776. My mother,
Elizabeth McLaurine; my sister, Elizabeth Blakley McLaurine; my

brother, Joseph; my brother, James Leveridges; my sister, Janett;
rest of my estate to my mother; monies I may be entitled to by
the will of my grandmother Catherine Blaikley(?). Exrs.: my
mother, Elizabeth McLaurine and Uncle Thompson Swann. Wit.:
Samuel Stegar, Elizabeth Davenport (X).

Catherine McLaurine (X)

Page 211: Appraisal of estate of DAVID WINNIFORD in obedience
to order of court, 22 January 1776. By: Adcock
Hobson, William Hobson, Job Johnson. Court 26 February 1776.

Page 212: Inventory of estate of LEANDER HUGHES taken June 28,
1776. By: Charles Anderson, John Woodson, Jr., Moore
Lumpkin. Court 22 April 1776.

Page 213: Appraisal of estate of JOHN COOK in obedience to court
order 26 February 1776. Court 22 April 1776.

Page 123: Appraisal of estate of JACOB MICHAUX. By: Jas. Bagby,
Edward Cox. Court 22 April 1776.

Page 215: Appraisal of estate of EDWARD MATHIAS in obedience to
order of court 24 January 1776. By: John Seay,
Zachariah Handrake, William Glen, Elizabeth Mathias (X). Court
22 April 1776.

Page 216: Will of WILLIAM POWELL, dated March 4, 1776, Pro.
22 April 1776. Wife, Martha; to my daughter, Bettey,
as follows to-wit: Liverpool and Henry and also a deed of gift
by William Cox acknowledges in Cumberland court of tract and
five negroes and all emoluments there from. Exrs.: friends,
Joseph Cox and Simon Gentry and Wm. Jones. Wit.: Will. Jones,
Susannah Ball of Buckingham County, Mary Moore.

Page 217: Inventory and appraisal of estate of WILLIAM POWELL.
Taken May 3, 1776. By: William Hudgens, Francis
Flippen, Richd. Richardson. Court 27 May 1776.

Page 218: Inventory and appraisal of estate of DAVID PARKER.
Taken May 24, 1776. John Flippin, Frances Flippin,
Christopher Robinson. Court 27 May 1776.

Will of PETER DAVIS, date March 26, 1776, Pro. 27 May
1776. Three brothers, Walter, Joel and Littleberry,
all my wearing apparel; my sister, Polly Davis, all my estate not
before mentioned, the said estate to be sold by my executors and
the money arising from all to be paid my said sister after all
debts are paid. Ex.: Robert Smith. Wit.: Charles Woodson,
Thomas Strange (X).   Peter Davis (X)

Will of PETER DEPP, dated April 2, 1774, Pro. 22 July
1776. All my estate to Jane Lester of Chesterfield
County on condition that she live with me during my natural life
and take care of my body and estate as far as her abilities will
with reason intend and not otherwise. Wit.: Ann A. Ashcraft(?),
Jacob Ashcraft(?), Richard Ashwiss(?) (X), John Ellis (X).

Will was presented by Jane Depp and Jane Lester as last writing
of Peter Depp. Jane Depp and Jane Lester, widow of Peter Depp
agreed to abide by the will.

Page 220: Will of SARAH BADGET, date May 1, 1775, Pro. 22 July
1776. My sister, Juda Badget, all my part of the

estate. Wit.: Susanna Martin (X), Ann Webster (X). The non-cupative will of Sarah Badget was proved by John Webster, Susanna Martin and Ann Webster.

Page 220: Will of BENJAMIN HARRIS of the Mannican town, dated 24 April 1776, Pro. 23 September 1776. Wife, Priscilla land whereon I now live that lies above the line running from the river known to be the dividing line between the lands I purchased of James Sublet and Peter David during her life and no longer; my two sons; son, Benjamin Harris, land I now live on containing about 1400 a., the use of the part allotted to my wife; to son, William Wager, all my lands on the James River and Salley's creek in Chesterfield and Cumberland Counties and all I purchased of John Roberts, Daniel Easley, Edward Hill and Sion Spencer with 51 a. I had of Abraham Sally also tract granted by patent situated in Chesterfield County; daughter, Mary Spencer; oldest daughter, Phebe; daughter, Edith; daughter, Sarah; daughter, Nancy; Henson (?) Wager Mosely(?) (this was not plain). Exrs.: Abraham Salle, Edward Moseley, Samuel Nivins, Bernard Markham. Wit.: Samuel Bellamy, William Kerr (X), George Shelton (X).
Benjm. Harris L.S.

Page 223: Appraisal of estate of JACOB FARIS. By: Wm. Taylor, Daniel Mosby, Robert Taylor, Wm. L. Smith.

Page 223: Account of administration of estate of WILLIAM WEATHER-FORD. By: Richard Weatherford, Thos. Davenport, Adcock Hobson, Frederick Hatcher. Court 6 August 1776.

Page 224: Will of JOHN NOELL of Littleton Parish, date 19 November 1776, Pro. 25 November 1776. Son, John Noel; daughter, Rebecca. Ex.: son, John Noel. Wit.: John Andrews, Benjamin Homesley, Larkin Smith. John Noel L.S.

Page 224: Will of ROBERT SMITH of Southam Parish, date 24 August 1771, Pro. 25 November 1776. My loving wife, Elizabeth; child I believe my wife is now pregnant with; son, Robert Smith; son, George Smith; son, Larkin Smith; son, Byrd Smith; daughter, Mary Smith; daughter, Betty Smith. Ex.: my wife, Elizabeth Smith and Samuel Hanes and Mark Andrews. Wit.: John Noell, Jesse Andrews, John Noell, Mary Andrews (X).

Page 224: Appraisal and inventory of JOSIAH WALTON in obedience of court of 23 September 1776. By: William Hudgens, David Douglass, Charles Parker. Court 27 January 1777.

Page 226: Inventory of THOMAS DAVENPORT. Court 23 December 1776. Thos. Davenport, Henry Davenport.

Note: Some records were repeated on this reel (microfilm).

Page 227: Appraisal of estate of JAMES DAY. By: William Dillon, Daniel Johnson, Robt. Farlong. Court 24 March 1777.

Page 229 - 230: Will of ANDREW AMONETT, date 28 February 1776, Pro. 24 March 1777. Sisters, Elizabeth and Magdalene, 100 a. land given me by my father adjoining Major Salle, widow Sowell my mother and John Amonette, Jr. to be equally divided between them; to my two sisters, all the money I have due me in hands of Anthony Martin. Exrs.: Anthony Martin, Brother William Amonett. Wit.: Francis Merriman, John Harris, Henry Holman.
Andrew Amonett

Appraisal of estate of PETER DAVIS and Inventory. By:
Francis McCraw, John Barnes, Stephen Pankey. Court
24 March 1777.

Page 229: Appraisal of estate of ROBERT SMITH. By: Henry Macon,
Bernard Gaines, John Slaughter. Court 24 March 1777.

Page 230: Will of AARON BUTLER, dated 13 October 1776, Pro.
24 March 1777. Wife, all my estate during her life
and afterwards I desire that the land whereon I now live to be
equally divided between my son John Butler and son Edmond Butler
and that the rest be divided among my four children, Frances
Puckett, Sarah Williams, John Butler, Edmond Butler. Exrs.:
John Woodson and John Holman. Wit.: John Raine, Matthias
Williams, David Puckett (X). Aaron Butler L.S.

Page 231: Will of JOHN HOBSON of Southam Parish, date 26 December 1771, Pro. 27 March 1777. Daughter, Drucilla
Thomson; daughter, Susanna Mosby; daughter, Nancy Hobson; son,
John Hobson, 400 a. of land whereon I now live, also all the land
adjoining thereto of the tract I purchased of Gideon Patterson
within a new marked line from my corner road oak from old field
known by the name of Yorkes the said line made in presence of
Field Robertson, Senr., Nicholas Mosby, Field Robenson, Jun. and
Jos. Robertson, also six negroes; son, William Hobson, part of
land I now live on beginning at my corner red oak then along a
new marked line to the creek thence up the creek to the land
thence to the beginning of said land marked in presence of Field
Robertson, Sr., Field Robertson, Jr., Nicholas Mosby and Joseph
Robertson; son, Thomas Hobson, land and plantation in Buckingham
County, also 150 pounds. I will that my children be kept together till they are grown; wife, Sarah Hobson during her life; my
son, John Hobson; I desire land in Henrico County to be sold; I
desire my executors to hire out my negro man Stephen; my daughters, Sarah, Nancy, and three sons, William, Thomas and John; I
desire Nicholas Mosby be hired to live on my plantation. Exrs.:
my wife, friends, William Hobson and Nicholas Mosby and Frederick
Hatcher. Wit.: Archibald Hatcher, Jno. Overton, Henry Hatcher.

Page 236: Appraisal of estate of JAMES SOUTHALL. By: Pauline
Anderson, William Wood, John Green. Court Order
28 October 1776, Court 28 April 1777.

Page 234: Appraisal of estate of ANDREW AMONETT. By: John
Bailey, Robert Wooldridge, Edward Wooldridge. Ex.:
Court 26 May 1777.

Page 234: Appraisal of estate of JOHN NOEL. By: John Slaughter,
Benjamin Sims, Joseph Chaffin. Court 26 May 1771.

Page 236: Will of EDWARD LIPFORD, date 20 March 1776, Pro.
28 April 1777. Sister, Nancy Lipford estate left me
by my grandfather, John Traylor of Chesterfield County. Ex.:
Cary Harrison, Amos Lipford. Wit.: Henry Bell, James Aiken.

Appraisal of estate of JOHN PHELPS taken June 4, 1777.
By: John Barnes, John Webster, Poindexter Mosby.
Court 23 June 1777.

Appraisal of estate of EDWARD LIPFORD.

Page 240: Will of DARBY FARLINES, dated 4 April 1777, Pro.
26 May 1777. My land on Tarwallet(?) River to be

equally divided between my four sons, John, Noble, William and Joseph, only my wife to have it during her life; my wife, Elizabeth; my three children, David Blanks, Jane and Peter Farlines; daughter-in-law, Lucy Pollock. Exrs.: John James Woodson of Woodfin, Robert Gordan, Peter Pollock.

Inventory of estate of JOHN HOLMAN taken 29 June 1777. Sarah Hobson, Nicholas Hatcher.

Inventory of JNO. HOLAND, deceased, in Buckingham County taken 1 July 1777. Nicholas Mosby, Frederick Hatcher. Court 24 November 1777.

Page 241: Inventory of estate of NEHEMIAH GLENN. Thomas Wright, Griffin Wright, James Glenn, Sr. Court 24 November 1777.

Page 242: Will of ALLEN CRIDDLE of Littleton Parish, date May 5, 1777, Pro. 26 January 1778. Wife, Ann Criddle, whole estate and at death of my wife to my several children: son, John; my several children. Exrs.: my wife and son, John. Wit.: Thos. J. Hill, Isaac Beacham, William Hill.

Allen Criddle (X)

Appraisal of estate of MATTHEW DAVIS. Jno. Matthews, Edward Scruggs, Jno. Jefferson. Court 26 January 1778.

Page 236: Appraisal of estate of EDWARD LIPFORD. Gerrand Ellyson, John Colquitt, William Colquitt. Court Order 28 April 1777.

Page 236: Will of JAMES BROWN of Littleton Parish, dated 16 November 1776, Pro. 28 July 1777. Wife, Mary Brown; eldest son, John; sons, James and Zachariah and Gideon and Randolph and Isham and Jak and Wilson, 1 sh. each; son, George; daughter, Susannah, Sarah, Hannah, Agness and Tabitha; after decease of my wife, Mary, or marriage, moveable estate to be divided between four of my children: Isham, Jak, Ulan(?) Pearson (not plain) and Lucy Brown. The land and plantation whereon I live I desire be equally divided between my son George Brown's two sons, George Brown and Archibald Brown. Exrs.: John Holeman, John Lee. Wit.: Hartwell Macon, Bartlett Angles, James Corley.

James Brown (X)

Page 237: Will of MATTHEW DAVIS, Southam Parish, date 4 April 1777, Pro. 27 October 1777. My three sisters, Easter Morgan, Elizabeth Davis and Ann Davis all my estate. Exrs.: Walter Davis and Jesse Thomas. Wit.: Mary Stevenson, Agnes Stegar (X), Margaret Stevenson.

Page 241: Will of WILLIAM ANGELLA, SR., date 7 December 1769, Pro. 26 January 1778. Son, William; son, Benjamin; son, Nicholas; son, James and his son, William; son, Joseph; daughter, Elizabeth Durham; daughter, Mary Genings and her children; daughter, Agness Basham and her children; my wife, Catherine; son, Bartlett. Exrs.: my wife and son, Bartlett. Wit.: Henry Macon, Francis Hobson, Joseph Hood.

Page 242: Inventory of estate of BENJAMIN HARRIS (Late of King William Parish). Taken by: Abraham Salle, Edward Moseley, Samuel Nivins, Barnard Markham. Court 23 January 1778.

Page 243: Inventory of estate of JOSEPH MOSBY. Taken Septem-

66

ber 19, 1775. By: William Tucker, John Moss, Thomas Tucker. Court 23 February 1778.

Will of JOHN MARTIN of Littleton Parish, date 3 January 1777, Pro. 23 March 1778. My cousin, Stephen Martin, son of Benjamin Martin, plantation whereon I now live and half of adjoining land; to Martin Dowdy, son of Richard Dowdy, the other half; rest of my estate to be sold and equally divided between all my brothers and sisters. Exrs.: my loving brothers, Ben, James and Martin. Wit.: Adcock Hobson, Edward Hobson, Lucy Hobson.

Page 245: Will of THOMAS MONDAY, dated 5 April 1777, Pro. 25 May 1778. To Martha Spears and her heirs, 40 lbs. Ex.: Nicholas Spears. Wit.: Jesse Thomas.

Page 245: Will of THOMAS MINTER, dated 11 March 1778, Pro. 27 July 1778. Mother, Mary Minter; my sisters, 100 lbs. now at interest in hands of Robert Dugles, Sen.; sister, Mary Minter; sister, Elizabeth Minter; sister, Nancy Montor; sister, Beccy Mintor; to brother, Joseph Mintor, the whole of my shoemakers tools; to brother, Simon Mintor. Ex.: Simon Hughes. Wit.: William Mintor, Jno. Flippen.
                                        Thomas Mintor L.S.

        Appraisal of estate of JOHN JONES. By: John Bagby, Robt. Dickenson, Thomas Tyrel. Court 27 July 1778.

Page 246: Appraisal of estate of THOMAS MONTAGUE. 22 August 1778 sworn to by: Edward Walton, Martin Richardson, Samuel Atkinson.

Page 247: Appraisal of estate of ALLEN CRIDDLE. By: Thos. Sugt. Hill, Jno. Jefferson, Chas. Parker. Court 24 August 1778.

        Appraisal of estate of THOS. MINTOR. William Hudgens, David Douglas, Francis Flippen. Court 24 August 1778.

Page 247: Court order to appraise estate of JOHN MARTIN. By: Joseph Hubbard, Thomas Moore, Lewis Grong(?). Court 23 November 1778.

Page 248: Account of administration of estate of SAMUEL ALLEN. By: Samuel Allen, ex. Sworn to by Samuel Allen and Jane Moss. Court 26 April 1779.

        Inventory of estate of THOMAS MUNDAY. William ...., Micajah Sinkeler, Joseph Baughan. Court 26 April 1779.

Page 250: Will of WILLIAM ADAMS of Littleton Parish, date 11 March 1778, Pro. 24 May 1779. Wife, Citta(?) Adams, all my estate until my youngest child comes of age 21 and when my son, John arrives to age of 21, my will is that my estate be divided equally among all my children: Martha, James, Stephen, Nathan, Mary, Elisha, William and John. Exrs.: Benjamin Wilson, Moses Arnold, Benjh. Thomas. Wit.: John Seay, James Garrett, William Garrett.   William Adams (X)

Page 250: Will of WILLIAM HAMBLETON, dated 27 September 1778, Pro. 23 August 1779. Wife, Ann; son, James, when he reaches age 21, my 400 acres on Little .... Creek; son, William Terry Hambleton, when he reaches 21, my 250 a. in Halifax County;

son, John Mosby Hambleton, all my land whereon I now live when he reaches 21 years; my children: Mary Sims, Elley Hambleton, and Lucy Hambleton, William Terry Hambleton and Susanna Hambleton and John Mosby Hambleton; I desire that Benjamin Hendrick have title to 150 a. in Amelia County which I have sold him and have not yet executed the deed to. Exrs.: my wife Ann and my son-in-law, John Sims and Frederick.... Wit.: William Davenport, Joseph Jenkins, Ann Davenport. Signed William Hambleton (X)

Page 252: Will of WILLIAM MAJOR now of Cumberland County, date 24 May 1778, Pro. 23 August 1779. Sister, Ann Major, 1/3 part of estate; brother, George Major, the remainder; my mother. Ex.: my brother, George Major. Wit.: Frederick Hatcher, Elizabeth Hatcher.

Page 253: Will of ADCOCK HOBSON of Littleton Parish, date 5 May 1779, Pro. 27 September 1779. Wife, Joanna Hobson; son, Thomas Hobson, land in Buckingham County; son, William Hobson; son, Caleb Hobson; son, Lawson Hobson; daughter, Winniferd Carter; daughter, Lucy Hobson; daughter, Elizabeth Hobson; daughter, Eliza Hobson; god daughter, Joanna White, 2 years substance in the family as long as her Aunt and God Mother thinks proper to keep her but if her father thinks proper to take her away before she can have her schooling, the estate to be clear of the charge. Exrs.: my wife, Joanna and sons, Thomas Hobson and William Hobson and my son, Caleb Hobson. Wit.: Frederick Hatcher, Isaac Beacham, Job Johnson.

Page 253: In obedience to court order of 27 September 1779, Appraisal of estate of JACOB HOBSON. Josiah Thomson, Creed Haskins, Rich'd. Booker. Court 25 October 1779.

Page 257: Account of administration of estate of JONAS MEADOR. By: Jehu Meador, admin. paid: to James Holloway for his account; to Richard James for his account; to James Holloway on account of Lewis Turner, orphan of Micajah Turner; to William Hill account, Drury Hudgens; paid Thomas Holand for his account; paid Sam Holloway for account of Jesse Boatright; Wm. Saunderson for finishing the crop; James Minter for his account; John Creasy for his account; Richard Blands account; Caleb Hughes for Thos. Kevil for work don; Zach McGwin for account James Guilliam; Jesse Meador for his account; Wm. Hughes for account Randolph Robinson; Holloway Hudgens for account Robert Hudgens; Wm. Hix for Jonas Meador bond on Joel Meador; paid James Holloway on account Lewis Turner estate; James Holloway on same account; Dal Boatright for his account; John Murry for bond of Jane Meador; paid Wm. Edwards for his account; Hezekiah Bradley for account of John Burton; George Carrington for account of Wm. Holland; Joseph Palmore for his account; Alex and Peterfield Trent and Co. for....accounts; Daniel Bates for account; Richard Crump; Miller Burford; Thos. Sugt. Hill; paid Hannah Holloway for his account; James Minter for Sarah Meador, orphan of Jonas Meador; Thomas Kevil for board and clothing of Ann Meador; Jesse Thomas; Bond vs. Caleb Hughes, 1773; Bond vs. Thomas Hughes, 1773; Micajah Compton and his wife; Thomas Kevil; due Lewis Turner, orphan of Micajah. In obedience to order of court account was dated 23 November 1778. Account examined and ordered recorded 18 October 1779.
Jos. Carrington

Page 259: Account of administration of THOS. SUGT. HILL. By: William Armistead. Mentions board and clothing of Thadeus Armistead, Mary Armistead, Nancy Armistead, Fanny Armistead, Joanna Armistead. Court 24 April 1780. Geo. Carrington,

Jos. Carrington. Further account of John Armistead, Court 24 April 1780.

Page 261: Estate of THOS. MONTAGUE by Jane Montague. Court
        10 February 1780 by Thos. Sug. Hill, Wm. C. Hill,
Jesse Thomas.

Page 262: Account of administration of estate of CHARLES BALLOW
        with Edward Hopkins, exr. Returned by: Henry Skip-
with, Richard Allen, Henry Macon. Court 26 June 1780.

Page 264: Will of CHARLES WINNIFORD, date 13 July 1780, Pro.
        24 July 1780. Wife....; daughter, Wilmoth; son,
George. Exrs.: wife and Jacob McGehee. Wit.: Nich. Goode, Wm.
Allen, Jno. Turner(?).   Charles Winniford (X)

        Inventory of estate of AARON BUTLER taken by: George
        Wright, Wm. Anderson, John Wright, Miller Woodson.
8 May 1777. Court 24 July 1780.

Page 265: Inventory of estate of CHARLES WINNIFORD taken by:
        Wm. Meredith, Matthew Nelson, Matthew Nelson, Warren
Walker. August 19, 1780. Court 28 August 1780.

Page 266: Will of HANNAH HOLLOWAY, date May 9, 1777, Pro. 28 Aug-
        ust 1780. Granddaughter, Hannah Spiers Holloway. Ex.:
James Minter. Wit.: Thos. Sugt. Hill, Moses Hubbard.

Page 266: Will of FRANCES MEADOR, dated 17 August 1774, Pro.
        25 September 1780. Daughter, Ann; granddaughter,
Rosannah Meador; my children, Joel Meador, Mary Holland, Frances
Holloway, John Meador, Josiah Meador, Jehu Meador, Jacob Meador
and Jesse Meador. Exrs.: Joel Meador, Jehu Meador and Jesse
Meador. Wit.: John Atkinson, Josiah Robertson, Meatha Meador
(X). Proved by Josiah Robertson and Meatha Meador. Samuel
Holloway and Simon Gentry were security for Jehu.

Page 267: Will of MATTHIAS WILLIAMS, dated 5 September 1780,
        Pro. 23 October 1780. Wife, Jane; my eight children:
Sarah, Elizabeth, Thomas, Matthias,Keziah, John, Susanna and
William. Ex.: son, Matthias Williams. Wit.: Joseph Michaux,
Elizabeth Williams (X), Keziah Williams.

Page 268: Will of THOMAS DAVENPORT, dated 30 March 1777, Pro.
        27 November 1780. Daughter, Anne Woodson, land in
Halifax County; son, Thomas Davenport, land in Halifax County;
wife, Lucy, my tract of land in Halifax County; granddaughter,
Lucy Woodson; grandson, Joseph Woodson. Exrs.: my wife and
sons, Thomas Davenport and son-in-law, John Woodson. Wit.:
William Hambleton, Henry Davenport, John Davenport.

Page 269: Appraisal of estate of MATTHEW WILLIAMS. Certified
        16 December 1780 by: Miller Woodson, John Holman,
George Wright.

Page 269: Appraisal of estate of FRANCES MEADOR. Court 22 Jan-
        uary 1781. 1 negro woman named Milla, L 600, 1 boy
Isaac, L 1000, L 7000.00; 1 negro man Harry, 2500.00; 1 old bay
horse, L 200, 1 calf, L 300, 500.00; 1 calf, L 300, one cow
L 300, one year old, 600.00; 1 sow and 5 pigs, one...., 150.00;
1 sow and 4 pigs, L 75, 4 sheats, L 200, 275.00; 1 L 20 half of
which is to the estate of each, 160.00; 2 beds and furniture,
L 500 each, 1005.00; 1 bedstead and 1 large trunk, 350.00; 2 pair

old cotton cards, flax wheel, 9 bottles, piggs, coffee pot, 2 mugs, 1 pepper box, 1 chamber pott, parcel of old pewter, 1 iron pit, 1 loom, 20 bushels corn, 1 woman saddle, etc.... Creed Haskins, Field Robinson, William Frayser.

Page 270: Inventory of estate of MARGARET HOLLAND by James Holloway, admr. Court 26 February 1781.

Page 271: Inventory and appraisal of estate of THOMAS WRIGHT.
Taken by William Anderson, Samuel Williams and Miller Woodson. Court 28 May 1781.

To Mr. Jessey Woodson in Bucking. County. North Carolina Caswell County, March 7, 1781. Dear Uncle Jessey. This comes to inform you that we are all well and about 15 miles in from our grand army and we are informed that the army are surrounded by our army we expect to join the grand army by the 10th of this month I do not know when I shal be back if ever Pray if I never come back sell as much as will pay my debts and the remainder I desire shall be given to my sister Polly and if I never return I bid you all farewell and if I do the....my portion therefore beg and intrust in your prayers and remember my love unto to Mary Ann Price no more at present by remember your loving friend.   Josiah Woodson

Court 28th March 1781, will of JOSIAH WOODSON was presented and letters of administration were granted to Jesse Woodson with George Carrington as security.

Page 72: Will of LAWRENCE ANDERSON, February 23, 1781, Pro. 28 May 1781. My wife, Rhoda; my desire is that my children be kept together and maintained and educated according to the discretion of my executors and after the death of my wife be sold to highest bidder and the money divided equally among all my children (not named). Executors: my brother, William Anderson and James Hudgens. Wit.: John Anderson, James Blanton, Drury Lacy.   Lawrence Anderson

Page 272: Will of JOSHUA DOSS of Littleton Parish, dated November 2, 1780, Pro. 28 May 1781. Wife, Elizabeth; son, James Doss; granddaughters, Nancy Stewart and Rebeccah Stewart; three sons, William, James and Joshua Doss; daughter, Lucy Loyd. Exrs.: James Doss, Joseph Jenkins. Wit.: Bartlet Thomson, Ann Hambleton (X), Polly Hambleton.   Joshua Doss (X)

Page 273: Will of WILLIAM SAUNDERSON, SR., dated 21 April 1781, Pro. 28 May 1781. Wife, Ann Saunderson; son, William Saunderson at my wife's death or marriage, land on North West side of Willises creek and as much on the other side thereof as shall make it square, the line to extend from the line of Drury Woodson, to the line of Jonas Meador, deceased; my two sons, Daniel and Robert Saunderson; my several children, Sarah Foster, John Saunderson, Nancy Foster, William Saunderson, Mary, Lucy, Daniel, Robert and Elizabeth (under 20); daughter, Susannah. Exrs.: my wife and Thos. Suggitt Hill. Joel Meggs, Nicholas Faulkner (X).   Signed Wm. Saunderson

Account of estate of WILLIAM POWEL, deceased, by Simon Gentry. By: Thos. Sugt. Hill, Frederick Hatcher. 23 November 1780. Court June 25, 1781.

Page 276: Estate of WILLIAM POWEL, deceased. Vouchers of Josiah Cox, executor of estate of Wm. Powel examined and approved at Court 25 June 1781.

Appraisal of estate of JOSIAH WOODSON. By: Sam'l.
Taylor, Drury Woodson, Orson Martin, John Melton.
Court 23 July 1781.

Page 277: Will of MATTHEW NELSON of Littleton Parish, dated
31 March 1781, Pro. 23 July 1781. Daughter, Betty
Owen; daughter, Dorothy Hundley; son, Ambrose Nelson; daughter,
Rachel Wright; son, Humphrey Nelson, land in Prince Edward co.;
daughter, Mary Nelson; daughter, Sarah Nelson; son, Andrew Nelson;
beloved wife, Mary Nelson. Ex.: two sons, Ambrose and Andrew
Nelson. Wit.: Henry Macon, Warren Walker, Sr., Richard Webber.

Page 278: Will of MARY ALLEN of Littleton Parish, dated 2 October 1778, Pro. 27 August 1781. Sister, Sarah Allen,
land and plantation I now live on and at her death to Nancy Allen
Handcock and if the said Nancy Allen Handcock should die without
heirs I give the same land to Isaac Allen, son of John Allen.
Ex.: my sister, Sarah Allen. Wit.: Joseph Jenkins, Lucy Jenkins (X), Francis Childress.   Mary Allen (X)

Page 278: Will of ROBERT SCRUGGS, dated 21 August 1780, Pro.
24 September 1781. Wife, Tabitha Scruggs; my seven
children: Nancy, Dick, Molly, Jesse, John Lumkin Scruggs, Robert,
and Sally; my mother, Ann Scruggs; daughter, Jemimah Frazer;
daughter, Theat(?); to my sons, Dick and John, land I purchased
of Hughes exrs. Muddy Creek; to son, Jesse Scruggs, land on
South side of Muddy Creek I purchased of Jacob and Isaac Winfree;
to Robert, land on North side of Muddy Creek I purchased of Jacob
and Isaac Winfree. Exrs.: wife, Tabitha Scruggs, Frederick
Hatcher, Simon Gentry. Wit.: Neil Thompson, John Holt, Creed
Haskins.

Page 280: Will of RICHARD PRICE, dated 23 March 1781, Pro.
22 October 1781. Wife, Mary, all the negroes also my
part of negroes arising from my father's estate; my two children,
Polly and William Price; my land in Halifax County to be sold.
Ex.: James Dejarnett, Joseph Dejarnett, Seymor Scott, Joseph
Michaux, William Anderson, my wife. Wit.: John Venable, Charles
Anderson, Isham Richardson.   Richard Price

Page 281: January 11, 1781. JAMES FOSTER desires that if he
should die before he returns from his tour of duty,
his wife is to have all his estate.
James Foster

Court held 22 October 1781, will presented by Sarah Foster and
letters of administration were granted to her.

Page 281: Will of WILLIAM HUDGENS, dated 26 August 1781, Pro.
22 August 1781(?). My four children: John, Jean,
Polly and Sally Hudgens; my brother, James to have care of John,
Jean and Sally (?); daughter Sally to be in care of Mary Merry-
man till she comes of age; James Hudgens to live on the planta-
tion and take charge of my three children. Ex.: my brother,
James Hudgens. Wit.: Edward Robinson, Robert Flippen, Jno.
Flippen.

Page 282: Appraisal of estate of LAURENCE ANDERSON. By: John
Langhorne, George Anderson, Thos. Holland. Court
26 November 1781.

Will of THOMAS HILL, dated 27 March 1779, Pro. 26 November 1781. As touching such estate as I am entitled to under will of my father, Joseph Hill, I give as follows: my brother, William Hill (under 20); my brother, Joseph Hill. Ex.: father-in-law, Daniel Allen. Wit.: Drury Lacy, Moses Allen.

Appraisal of estate of ROBERT SCRUGGS. By: Francis Flippen, Simon Hughes, William Minton. Court 28 January 1782.

Page 284: Appraisal of estate of JOSHUA DOSS. By: Moses Arnold, Robt. Noell, William Allen. Court 28 January 1782.

Appraisal of estate of MARY ALLEN, deceased. By: Moses Arnold, Robert Noell, Bartlett Thomson. Court 28 January 1782.

Page 285: Will of JOHN JOHNS, dated 20 June 1781, Pro. 28 January 1782. Wife, Martha Johns. Ex.: Robert Johns. Wit.: Jesse Johns, Thos. Nunnally, Richd. North (X).

Page 285: Will of BENJAMIN WALKER, dated 9 November 1781. Daughter, Mary Walker; daughter, Betsy Walker; daughter, Judah Walker; wife, Sarah Walker; daughter, Magdalene Walker under age. Ex.: wife, Sarah and William, son of Warren Walker. Wit.: John Holman, Warren Walker, Sr., Wm. Walker, son Wm. Walker.
Benjamin Walker (X)

Page 286: Appraisal of estate of THOS. DAVENPORT. Bartlet Thomson, George Woodson, Jacob Ferris, Moses Arnold. Court 28 January 1782.

Page 287: Appraisal of estate of BENJAMIN WALKER. Certified under our hands: John Holman, George Wright, Warren Walker, Sr. Court 23 February 1782.

Page 288: Appraisal of estate of WILLIAM SAUNDERSON. John Jefferson, James Austin, Nicholas Faulkner (X). Court 25 February 1782.

Page 289: Inventory of estate of MATTHEW NELSON. Exhibited and ordered recorded Court 25 February 1782.

Will of HENRY FARMER of Littleton Parish, dated 1 April 1781, Pro. 25 March 1782. Wife, Catherine; at death of my wife, estate to be equally divided between Mary Ann Elson's two twin daughters named Martha and Mary. Exrs.: friends, Frederick Hatcher and Thomas Nash. Wit.: Judith Starkey, Joseph Starkey, Thomas Caldwell.
Henry Farmer (X)

Page 290: Appraisers John Flippen, Francis Flippen and Simon Hughes appraised the estate of WILLIAM HUDGENS, deceased. Court 22 April 1782.

Page 291: Will of THOMAS TABB, dated 8 January 1782, Pro. 22 April 1782. Son, Edward Tabb; son-in-law, Robert Brown's children; my daughter, Walton; my daughter, Beatrite; my daughter, Douglas; daughter, Scruggs; daughter, Locky Cobb. Exrs.: Jesse Cobbs and my daughter, Lockey. Wit.: Adam Couzens.
Signed Thomas Tabb

Page 292: Inventory and appraisal of estate of RICHARD PRICE.
          Taken November 24, 1781. John Woodson, William Ander-
son, Samuel Williams. Court 12 April 1782.

Page 292: Will of NANCY BOND, dated 7 April 1782, Pro. 22 April
          1782. My mother, Anna Hubbard. Exrs.: Samuel Hollo-
way, William Brown. Wit.: Clement Brown, Wright Bond, Patte
Brown.

Page 293: Appraisal of estate of EDWARD ROBINSON, deceased, in
          obedience to order of 28 January 1782 by Creed Haskins,
Wm. C. or E. Hill, John Flippen. Estate totalled L 1269-16-0.

Page 294: Appraisal of estate in Halifax County of THOMAS DAVEN-
          PORT. By: Jeremiah Pate, John Irvine, James Irvine.
Court 27 May 1782.

Page 924: Will of THOMAS SUGGITT HILL, dated November 21, 1781,
          Pro. 24 June 1782. Grandson, Thos. Hobson Hill; my
children, Frances, Caley, Jesse, Thos. John and Betsy Hill;
daughter, Frances; Jesse Hill; wife, Betsy Hill; if any of my
children marry against will of their mother, that legacy is to
be in hands of my wife to give to such others of her children
(except Sarah Hill) as she may think fit; grandson Thos. Hobson
Hill; my three sons, Thos., Jesse and John; my daughter, Sarah
Hill, wife of Isaac Hill. Ex.: my wife and any person she may
make choice to assist her. Wit.: William Edwards, Andrew
Edwards, William Hammontree (X).   Thos. Sugt. Hill

Codicil: The child I have reason to believe my daughter-in-law
is now with, Sarah Hill, I desire that the three negroes given
to Thomas Hobson Hill be equally divided between Thomas and the
child to be born of my said daughter-in-law before 10 day May
1782. The same witnesses as to will.

          Appraisal of Estate of HENRY FARMER. Alex Gutthery,
          Theodorick Carter, George Woodson. Court 24 June 1782.

          Appraisal of estate of THOS. SMITH made 22 June 1782
          by Theod. Carter, Henry Davenport, George Woodson.

Page 297: Inventory of estate of THOMAS SUGGITT HILL. Taken
          22 July 1782. Betty Hill. Court 22 July 1782.

          Appraisal of estate of MOSES ALLEN. Nathan Glen,
          Thomas Wright, Nathan Womack. Taken and recorded.
Court 22 July 1782.

Page 298: DRURY SCRUGGS will, dated 29 April 1782, Pro. 26 Aug-
          ust 1782. Son, John; son, Theodorick; daughter, Jane
Easeley; son, Drury; son, Edward; daughter, Ann Minton; son,
Carter; daughter, Fanny Scruggs; wife to act as guardian to minor
Carter and if she die before son Carter I appoint son, Edward to
manage for him; beloved wife, Mary. Ex.: my wife, Mary Scruggs
son John and Edward Scruggs. Wit.: Will Anderson, Archibald
Hatcher, John L. Weed(?).   Drury Scruggs (X)

Page 299: Will of DANIEL JONES, dated 30 June 1782, Pro. 26 Aug-
          ust 1782. Wife, Judith; son, Daniel, land in New Kent;
my sons, Daniel, Fraderick and Waller(?); my daughters, Mary,
Sale, Beetsee(?) and Susanna. Ex.: Geo. Carrington, Jr.,
Samuel Taylor. Wit.: Richard Taylor, William Bond, Daniel Boatright.   Daniel Jones

Page 300: Appraisal of estate of NANCY BOND. Robert Noell, John Noell, Rob. Clopton.

Page 300: Will of GEORGE CHAMBERS of Littleton Parish, dated 19 January 1782, Pro. 23 September 1782. My kinswoman Elizabeth Hazlewood, all my estate. Ex.: Henry Macon. Wit.: Warren Walker, Sr., Andrew Nelson.

Page 310: Appraisal of estate of JEREMIAH TAYLOR. Edmund Forgeson, Jeremiah Parker, Hezekiah Robertson. Court 27 January 1783.

Page 310: Will of THOMAS WILLIAMS, dated 9 May 1782, Pro. 27 January 1783. Wife, Esther, all my part of my father's estate and all my right in the land Samuel Vawter now lives on. Ex.: friend, John Williams and John Morrow. Wit.: Frances McCraw, Anderson Cocke.

Page 311: Appraisal of estate of JOHN FURLONG. John Woodson, Richard Taylor, John Creasy. Court 28 April 1783.

Page 300-301: Will of JOHN VENABLE, dated 6 May 1782, Pro. 23 September 1782. Wife, Elizabeth Venable; son, Abraham Venable (under age); child my wife is now pregnant with; daughter, Martha Venable. Exrs.: Joseph Michaux, Charles Allen, Samuel Venable. Wit.: Ann Venable, Micajah Anderson, Jacob Venable.   Signed John Venable.

Appraisal of estate of THOMAS HARVEY. Given 2 October 1792 by: James Brown, William Brown, John Minter. Court 28 October 1782.

Page 302: Appraisal of estate of JOHN VENABLE. By: Thomas Anderson, William Anderson, Samuel Williams. Court 28 October 1782.

Page 302: Appraisal of estate of GEORGE CHAMBERS. 15 October 1782. Taken by: Philip Webber, Richard Webber, William Walker, William Walker, Sr. Court 28 October 1782.

Page 303: Appraisal of estate of DRURY SCRUGGS. Taken 16 November 1782 by: Phinebas Thomas, James Douglas, Jesse Boatright. Court 25 November 1782.

Inventory of estate of JAMES COCK. By: Archer Allen, Henry Martin (X), John Burton. Court 25 November 1782.

Page 304: Will of JAMES ANDERSON, dated 16 May 1782, Pro. 25 November 1782. Son, Thomas Anderson, the plantation whereon I now live, 400 a.; son, James Anderson, the plantation where Thomas Anderson now lives with 400 a. of land; daughter, Mary Pearce; daughter, Sarah Compton; daughter, Elizabeth LeGrand; daughter, Agnes Anderson, youngest and under age; grandson, James Pearce; wife, Betty Anderson; my five daughters. Exrs.: James Allen, Sr., Thomas Anderson. Wit.: William Anderson, Chas. Allen, Mary Sanders.   Signed Jas. Anderson

Page 306: Will of SAMPSON FLEMING, dated 17 June 1754, Pro. 23 December 1782. Unto Jane Scott, 75 a. in Cumberland County and bounded as follows: on Wm. Bond, Robt. Smith, John Chambers, John Pleasants, Jacob Winfrey, Wm. Hughes; if she die without heir begotten by a free born husband, the estate to go to her sister, Ann Scott; I bequeath to Ann Scott, mother of

Jane, her choice of cattle; I give my wife, Jane a slave belonging to John Merryman; what remains if any to be equally divided
between my children begot by my wife Jane belonging to John Merryman. Ex.:.... Wit.: Sack.... Whitebread, Wm. Moss.

Administration was granted to Francis Couzens.

Page 307: Appraisal of estate of WILLIAM HILL. By: Wm. C. Hill,
           Simon Hughes, Edward Clements. Court 23 December 1782.

Page 307: Will of SAMUEL BROWN, dated 18 July 1782, Pro. 23 Dec-
           ember 1782. Son, Clement Brown, all my land; daughter,
Martha Holland; all my children: Clement Brown, Sarah Winfree,
Mary Weatherford, Martha Holland, Elizabeth Smith, Nancy Brown
and Rachel Bradley. Ex.: Thos. Suggett Hill, Clement Brown.
Wit.: James Brown, William Brown, Lewis Turner, Wright Bond,
Hezekiah Bradley.   Samuel Brown L.S.

           Appraisal of estate of DANIEL JONES. Daniel Boatright,
           Drury Woodson, Jesse Woodson. Court 27 January 1783.

Page 309: Appraisal of estate of SAMUEL BROWN. Jehu Meador,
           Moses Hubbard, Wright Bond. Court 27 January 1783.

Page 311: Inventory of estate of THOS. WILLIAMS. Wm. Anderson,
           Anderson Cocke, Sam Williams. Court 28 April 1783.

Page 311-312: Inventory of estate of JAMES FOSTER. Thomas
           Green, Moses Levern. Taken 31 August 1782. Court
18 April 1783.

Page 312: Will of MARTAIN OSLIN, dated June 9, 1780, Pro.
           28 April 1783. I desire my brother Samuel Oslin to
have my part in my father's estate; my sister Mary Ann Oslin....
Ex.: Samuel Oslin. Wit.: Jesse Thomas, John Moreland.

           Will of JOSEPH PRICE, of Littleton Parish, dated
           23 October 1779. Son, Edmund; son, Joseph Shores
Price; grandson, Joseph Flippen; son, John Price; granddaughter,
Sukey Price, daughter of my daughter Hannah Armistead; wife, Ann
Price; grandson, Joseph, son of my sons Joseph Shores and Edmund
and to any son of my son John which shall be named Joseph; daugh-
ter, Mary Flippen, her son Joseph; each of my daughters, Eliza-
beth Rowlen(?), Ann Thomas, Judith Gunter and Sarah Palmers;
son-in-law, Phinebas Thomas; my daughters, Mary, Elizabeth, Ann,
Judith and Sarah; I desire George Carrington, Jr., George
Carrington, Samuel Taylor divide my slaves. Ex.: Samuel Taylor,
George Carrington, Jr.

Page 316: I am informed that my son-in-law Phinebas Thomas has
           said he intended to claim part of my estate under the
pretense of a promise of bonds or contracts in their favor by me
heretofore made that I do not recollect ever to have made any
promise which could entitle my son-in-law or any of my daughters
to demand any part of my estate. It is my will that if my said
sons-in-law and daughters or any of them under any such pretense
recover any part of my estate so much as he, or she or they shall
so recover shall be taken out of that part of my estate lent or
given in my said will to the wives of such sons-in-law or to
such daughters and their children. 15 January 1783. Wit.:
Samuel Atkinson, Samuel Atkinson, G. Carrington.
                              Joseph Price (X)

Page 315: Will of ZACHARIAH HENDRICK of Littleton Parish, dated
          9 January 1782, Pro. 26 May 1783. Wife, Elizabeth,
all my estate, after death or marriage, to my son; Elijah, all
my land whereon I live and if he dies without issue, I lend plantation to my son, James, and if he die without issue, desire the
land to be equally divided or sold and the money divided among
all my children then living: son, William, son, James, son,
Elijah, daughter, Elizabeth, daughter, Martha, daughter, Rebeckah,
my wife's mother. After the death of my wife, all the remainder
of my estate goods, chattels and effects to be divided equally
among my children then living. Ex.: my two sons, Obediah and
John and my wife, Elizabeth. Wit.: John Stanley, Wm. Richardson,
Pheby Richardson (X), Jonathan Taylor (X), Joseph Starkey.
                                        Zachariah Hendrick L.S.

Certificate of administration granted to Exrs. Securities:
Daniel Allen and Nathan Womack.

        Will of FREDERICK HATCHER of Littleton Parish, dated
          13 June 1782, Pro. 23 June 1783. Wife, Sarah; son,
John Hatcher; daughter, Susannah Hatcher; son, Benjamin Hatcher,
land joining Josiah Thomson and David Burton; son, Frederick
Hatcher; son, Henry Hatcher; daughters, Mary, Betty, Sarah, Nancy
and Lucy. Exrs.: my wife, Sarah Hatcher and son, John Hatcher.
Wit.: Francis McCraw, William Hobson, Dancy McCraw.
                                        Frederick Hatcher

Page 318: Inventory of estate of MARTIN OSLIN. Martin Richard-
          son, James Austin, John Criddle. June 20, 1783,
Court 24 June 1783.

        Will of HUMPHREY KEEBLE of Littleton Parish, dated
          8 July 1782, Pro. 24 June 1783. Unto Catherine Smith
during her life, one negro boy and one negro girl and after her
death to return to be divided with my other negroes; I lend unto
Katharine Boyd during her life, negro and at her death to return
to be divided; unto Sally Gwyn, one looking glass; unto Walter
Keeble, son of Dorothy Keeble and her heirs, the plantation
whereon I now live when he arrives to age of 21; to Walter Keeble,
son of Walter Keeble, the land and plantation whereon his father
Walter Keeble now lives known by the name of Hendricks when he
arrives to age of 21; unto Walter Keeble, son of Dorothy Keeble
and Walter Keeble, son of Walter Keeble, all my negroes with all
my personal estate when they arrive to age of 21. Exr.: Walter
Keeble, Sr. Wit.: Frederick Hatcher.
                                        Humphrey Keeble, L.S.

Page 319: Will of JAMES HOLLAND of Southam Parish, dated 15 July
          1783, Pro. 25 August 1783. Son, Jonas Meador Holland,
the tract of land containing 200 a. whereon he now lives; my
desire is that my son Jonas Meador take care of his mother and
sisters; my desire also is that such of my daughters as are under
age or unmarried as they come of age or marries, be furnished
with a feather bed and furniture and stock equal to such of my
children as are married to be given to them out of the profits
of my estate before a division be made to them; I lend unto my
wife, Mary, all the rest; my desire is that after the death or
marriage of my wife that all my land be sold and such money
arising be equally divided amongst my daughters or their heirs
with the money I have a right to under the last will of my wife's
father and mother. If my wife should marry, I desire she should
have everything coming or brought with her into my estate by
marriage and at her death divided as above mentioned. Ex.: son,

Jonas Meador Holland and son-in-law John Anderson. Wit.: Alsop
Taylor (X), Martha Holland (X), Francis Holland (X), Richd. Allen.
James Holland (X)

Page 322: Will of JOHN BRADLEY of Littleton Parish, dated 10 September 1782, Pro. 25 August 1783. Wife, Phebe Bradley;
son, William; son, John; son, Hezekiah; son, David Bradley; daughter, Joanna White; Mary Dunklan; Nancy Brown; my daughter, Sarah
Holland (?); daughter, Jenny Anderson. Ex.: John Meador, Simon
Gentry, Francis Flippen, Hezekiah Bradley. Wit.: Billey Holloway, Wm. C. Hill, Samuel Holloway.

Page 323: Inventory of estate of JAMES HOLLAND. Nathan Womack,
Daniel Allen, Jesse Anderson (X). Court 21 October
1783.

Page 326: Account of administration of estate of BENJAMIN WALKER.
By: William Walker. Some of the names that were
mentioned: Warren Walker, Sarah Walker, Jno. Holman, Susanna
Holman, William Walker, David Ross.... By: Miller Woodson,
John Woodson, John Holman. Court 22 September 1783.

Account of administration of estate of JOHN ARMISTEAD
with William Armistead, admt. Mentions boarding and
schooling two girls, Joanna and Fanny. George Carrington, Ben.
Wilson, Joseph Carrington. Court 29 September 1783.

Page 331: Inventory of estate of FREDERICK HATCHER. Court
10 August 1783.

Appraisal of estate of JOSEPH PRICE. James Austin,
Edmond Walton, Samuel Johnson, Martin Richardson.
Court 22 November 1783.

Page 332: Inventory of estate of HUMPHREY KEEBLE. Thomas Hobson,
John Woodson, Joseph Hubbard. Court 22 December 1783.

Page 333: Appraisal of estate of JOHN BRADLEY. Wm. Daniel,
Samuel Holloway, Jeffrey Robertson. Court 26 January
1783.

Page 337: Will of MARY HARRIS, dated December 4, 1783, Pro.
July 1784. Sister, Pamela MacRae; sister, Ann Kennon
Harris. Ex.: the Reverend Christopher MacRae. Test.: Codring-
ton Carrington, John Allen, George Carrington, son of Joseph.
Mary Harris

Page 339: Appraisal of estate of WILLIAM HAMBLETON. Josiah
Thomson, Chas. B. Allou(?), Moses Arnold. Court
29th May 1784.

Page 339: Estate of THOMAS HILL. Court 24 May 1784.

Will of JOHN LANGHORNE, dated 3 March 1784, Pro.
26 July 1784. (right hand side of this will is faded
out) My children: son, John, land in Kentucky, Elizabeth and
.... Langhorne, son, Maurice, wife, Sarah Langhorne. Ex.: my
wife and loving brother, Maurice Langhorne and Thomas Miller.
Test.: friend, Thomas Kennon Sizer(?), Edward Ferguson, Wm.
Martin, Mary Langhorne.

Page 341: Inventory of estate of JOHN LANGHORNE. Slaves, cattle,
sheep, household furniture, etc. (very pale and hard

to read) G. Keeling, Jeffrey Robertson, William Eagleston.
Court 26 July 1784.

Will of HANNAH SCRUGGS, date 17 May 1784, Pro. 25 October 1784. Sister, Cosiah Scruggs. Ex.: William....,
William Cunningham, sister, Coziah Scruggs. Wit.: John Hall
(could be Holt), Philip Hall, Elizabeth Cunningham, Susannah
Parker.   Hannah Scruggs (X)

Page 344: Inventory of negroes, etc. of estate of JACOB MICHAUX.
           Court October 25th, 1784.

           Appraisal of estate of JAMES BRADLEY (not clear).
           John ...., G. Ellison, William Edwards.

Page 346: Will of ABRAHAM SANDIFER, date 7 July 1784, Pro.
           22 November 1784. Wife, Joanna; each of my sons; my
son, Matthew; daughter, Dianna; daughter, Frances Smith. Ex.:
John Woodson, Stephen Cook and my wife. Wit.: Miller Woodson,
Sarah de Graffenried, Wm. Askew (X).

Page 348: Will of GEORGE CARRINGTON, dated...., Pro.....(right
           hand side faded out). Sons, Paul and George and
Joseph Carrington; son, Nathaniel; daughter, Mary Scruggs(?);
son-in-law, Nathaniel Cabell; son, Edward; son-in-law, John
Bernard and my daughter, his wife, land in Buckingham County;

Page 350: grandson, William Robert Bernard and George Bernard;
           whereas the George Carrington, the elder Esq., late
of County of Cumberland, died without having made a will so as
to legally dispose of his estate and having left a paper pro-
fessing to be his will his intentions are manifest for all the
children and all parties agree....Children: Paul, Joseph,
Nathaniel, John Carrington, his wife, Edward Carrington, Nicholas
Cabell for Hannah his wife and Joseph Watkins for Mary his wife
....reach an agreement; Mayo Carrington; John Bernard. Having
confidence in the integrity of Paul Carrington the older brother
and heir at law to....estate distribution....according to the
intention....

Page 355: districution of the estate by Paul Carrington. Court
           28 February 1785. Agreement to accept was signed by:
Jos. Carrington, Nath. Carrington, John Bernard for wife, Ed.
Carrington, N. Cabell for self and wife, Joseph Watkins for self
and wife. Wit.: John Carter, William Palmore, Will Cabell, Paul
Carrington.

Page 359: Paul Carrington relinquishes right to execute father's
           will. Wit.: Maurice Langhorne and Joseph Carrington.

Page 359: Appraisal of estate of ABRAHAM SANDIFER. John Holman,
           George Wright, Samuel Williams. Court 28 February
1785.

Page 359: Will of FIELD ROBINSON of Littleton Parish, date
           7 March 1785, Pro. 28 March 1785. Son, Daniel Robin-
son; son, William Robinson; son, Field Robinson; son, Joseph
Robinson; daughter, Temperance; daughter, Obedience Nichols, what
she has in her possession; daughter, Elizabeth Robinson, 50 a.
land, etc.; daughter, Judith; daughter, Nancy, what she has.
Ex.: Daniel Robinson, Field Robinson. Test.: Harrison Jones,
Keziah Robinson, Stephen Robinson.
                                        Field Robinson L.S.

Page 360: Appraisal of estate of EDMOND PEARCE. John Holman,
William Walker, Jr., Joseph Macon. Court 28 March
1785.

Account of administration of estate of GEORGE WRIGHT.
Names mentioned: George Wright, William Wright,
Arch'd. Wright, Gabriel Wright, Henry Wright, Sally Wright,
Thomas Wright. Distribution to legatees: George Wright, William
Wright, Archd. Wright, Thomas Wright, Gabriel Wright, Mary Wright,
Sarah Wright. Court 25 March 1785. Heirs George Wright. Under-
signed settled with Saymore Scott, Miller Woodson, John Woodson.

Page 366: Will of HENRY HARMAN of Littleton Parish, date 4 March
1785, Pro. 23 May 1785. My two sons, Edward and
Dangerfield Harman, land I formerly lived on; daughter, Tabitha
Harman. Ex.: my two sons, Edward and Dangerfield Harman. Wit.:
Wm. Ma uny(?), James Doss.

Page 369: Will of WILLIAM WOODSON, dated - no date, Pro. 27 June
1785. Son, Jesse Woodson; grandson, Drury Woodson,
son of Drury Woodson; grandson, William Woodson, son of Shaddrack
Woodson; to Drury and William, 125 a. part of a tract that I gave
to Shadrick. Ex.: Drury Woodson. Test.: Sam'l. Taylor, William
Harris (X), Mary Woodson.   William Woodson (X)

Page 370: Will of JOHN MERRYMAN, dated 3 April 1785, Pro. 27 June
1785. Wife, Mary Merryman; son, Thomas Merryman; son,
Ralph Merryman; it is my will and desire that the legacy left to
my wife, Mary Merryman father Ralph Flippen be equally divided
between my two sons, Thomas and Ralph after Martha Flippen's
death. Ex.: wife, Mary Merryman and friends, John Flippen and
William Cunningham. Wit.: David Carter (X), Robert Brown (X),
Jacob Flippen.   John Merryman

Page 372: Account of administration of estate of JAMES COCKE.
By: John Ford, adm. Examined by: John Lee, Robt.
Anderson, Archer Allen. Court 27 June 1785.

Page 375: Appraisal of estate of FIELD ROBINSON. By: Creek
Haskins, Thomas Ballew, Simon Gentry. Court 26 September 1786.

Page 374: Will of WILLIAM SCRUGGS, dated 17 May 1785, Pro.
25 June 1785. Son, John Scruggs, ½ land on Rock
Island Creek in Buckingham County and at death of my wife, the
other half to go to the two other sons; all personal estate to
my wife as long as she lives and at her death to be equally
divided between my daughters but one bed....son, John Scruggs.
Ex.: my wife and son, Edward Scruggs and Charles Woodson. Wit.:
Thos. Scruggs (X), Judy Scruggs (X), Edward Scruggs.
                William Scruggs (X)

Page 376: Will of JOHN BURTON of Littleton Parish, dated
9 March 1785, Pro. 26 September 1785. My three sons,
John, Allen and Benjamin, all my land in Pittsylvania County;
son, Jesse, land and plantation in Cumberland County on Little
Guinea Creek after the death of his mother, also one negro; son,
John, negro girl; son, Allen, negro boy; son, Benjamin, negro
boy; daughter, Nancy Burton, negro woman; daughter, Betsy, negro
girl; daughter, Susannah, negro girl and 500 pounds current
money; wife, Agnes Burton during her life all the rest of my
negroes; grandson, John Burton, son of Allen, 500 pounds current
money. Ex.: my wife, Agnes Burton, friends, Joseph Carrington,

and Frederick Hatcher. Wit.: Benjamin Allen, James Hudgens.
John Burton

Page 378: Will of HENRY MACON, date 9 October 1783, Pro. 24 October 1785. My wife during her natural life, the 21
following slaves....; likewise to my wife, the plantation whereon
I now live with 1455 acres of land and the use of my horses and
riding chair, etc.; to John Pleasants Woodson, son of Tucker
Woodson and his heirs after my wife's decease, two negroes; to
John Pleasants Woodson; to son, William, land after death of my
wife; to son, John, land lately purchased of Joseph Chaffin, also
negroes; to son, John Macon, 1435 acres on South side of Great
Guinea Creek being land my father gave me by his will. I declare
the provision made for my wife in this will to be full satisfaction for and in lieu of her dower. Ex.: sons, William and John
Macon and friend, George Carrington, Jr. Wit.: Larkin Smith,
James Doss, Bird Smith.   Henry Macon

Page 380: Appraisal of estate of JOHN MERRYMAN. By: John
Murry, William Forgerson, Thomas Flippen. Court
24 October 1785.

Appraisal of estate of JENNET STEGAR, deceased. By:
Samuel Atkinson, Martin Richardson, Samuel Osling.
Court 24 October 1785.

Page 382: Will of JOHN JONES of Littleton Parish, dated 30 October 1779, Pro. 28 November 1785. Wife, Sarah Jones;
lands to be equally divided between my two sons; bequeath to all
my children both sons and daughters to be equally divided, all
my estate not herein before disposed of except my daughter, Mary
Ann Jones who has received 237 acres of land which is to be
taken out of her part of my negroes, also one feather bed and
furniture, one saddle, two iron potts, etc. Ex.: son, Harrison
Jones, Anderson Hughes, Thomas Hobson. Wit.: Frederick Hatcher,
Benjamin Hatcher.   Signed John Jones

Page 384: Will of JOHN THOMSON, dated 5 October 1785, Pro.
26 December 1785. Wife, Elizabeth Thomson, all my
estate during her widowhood to have and enjoy for her support
and maintenance for boarding and schooling and cloathing of my
son, John Daniel Thomson till he arrive at the age of 21 but if
she should marry in that case I bequeath unto my said son, John
Daniel Thomson all my estate; my brother, William Morris Thomson.
Ex.: my father, Josiah Thomson and Thomas Nash. Wit.: Chrisr.
MacRae, Josiah Thomson, E. R. Swann.
John Thomson L.S.

Page 385: Appraisal and inventory of estate of JOHN JONES. By:
N. Patteson, Moses Arnold, George Woodfin.
Total L 2661-7-6. Court 23 January 1786.

Page 388: Inventory of estate of WILLIAM SCRUGGS. By: John
Price, Orson Martin, Benjamin Faris. Court 23 January 1786.

Page 389: Will of PHINEBAS GLOVER, dated 20 August 1786, Pro.
27 February 1786. My wife during her natural life,
slaves; son, Samuel Glover after death of his mother, the land
and plantation whereon I now live and after his decease to his
son, John Glover; Mary Robinson, one negro boy; to Lucy Taylor,
one negro girl; my grandson, John Glover; to Elizabeth Walker,
one negro boy; son, Robert Glover, two negroes; son, Phinebas

Glover. Ex.: Joseph Taylor, Samuel Taylor. Wit.: Richard
Taylor, James Isom (X), Daniel Jones.

Phinebas Glover (X)

Page 390: Account of administration of estate of HARRIS HAMMON-
TREE. By: Cary Harrison, George Keeling, W. Wilson.
Dated: Court 19 February 1786.

Page 391: Will of CHARLES ANDERSON, dated 26 August 1783, Pro.
27 February 1786. I have given to my daughter Keziah
Raine the part of my estate I intend to give to her; to my
daughter, Frances Redd; to my daughter, Elizabeth Wade; to my
daughter, Martin (Morton(?); son, William Anderson, land I now
live on, slaves; grandchildren: John Raine, Mary Ann Raine,
George Raine, Charles Raine, Joseph Shelton Raine, 5 pounds
apiece as they come of age; grandson, Charles Anderson, one negro
boy; granddaughter, Sarah Holcombe Anderson. Ex.: son, William
Anderson. Wit.: Samuel Williams, Benjamin Allen.

Charles Anderson

Page 392: Inventory and appraisal of estate of CAPT. JOHN BURTON.
By: John Ford, George Woodfin, Archer Allen. Court
27 March 1786.

Page 393: 26 June 1786. Letters of administration were granted
to Sarah Langhorne, executrix of will (see will page
339). Security, Henry Bell.

Page 395: Appraisal of estate of THOMAS JOHNS, deceased. By:
Nathan Womack, John Colquit, Daniel Allen. Returned
April 24, 1786. Court 26 June 1786.

Page 396: Appraisal of estate of JOHN FOLKS. By: William
Hobson, John Hobson, Drury Hatcher. Court 26 June
1786.

Page 397: Will of JOSIAH ROBINSON of Littleton Parish. Dated
23 January 1786, Pro. 26 June 1786. My mother, Judith
Robinson, 2 negroes Monday and Isaac during her natural life,
also 4 of the best of my hogs to her, after my mother's death, I
give to my brother, Jones Robinson one negro named Monday; after
my mother's decease I give to my two brothers, Edward Robinson
and Field Robinson one negro boy named Isaac; to my brother,
Field Robinson, my young sorrel mare, bridle and saddle; to my
brother, Edward Robinson, 4 head of my sheep; to my brother,
Jones, my old sorrel mare and her first colt. Exrs.: my two
brothers, Jones and Edward Robinson. Wit.: Moses Hubbard,
Wright Bond, Joseph Hubbard (X). Signed Josiah Robinson (X)

Page 399: Inventory and appraisal of slaves and personal estate
of GEORGE CARRINGTON, the elder, late of Cumberland
County. Taken 4 March 1785, Richard James, John Woodson, James
Gilliam. Court 26 June 1786.

Page 405: Appraisal of estate of WILLIAM EDWARDS. By: Jesse
Johns, John Colquit, Robert Colquit. Court 26 June
1786.

Page 405: Will of FRANCES MACON, relict of Henry Macon. Date
24 December 1785, Pro. 26 June 1786. To John P.
Woodson, son of Tucker Woodson, six of my slaves; to my good
friend the Rev. Christopher MacRae, all the rest of my slaves;
residue of my estate to Caty Todd Macon, son of John Macon and

81

her heirs in the male line that is in the line of her father's family. Ex.: Joseph Woodson, the Rev. Christopher McRae. Wit.: Jno. Macon, James Doss.

Page 406: Will of ELIZABETH OAKS, dated 6 July 1784, Pro. 26 April 1786. To Elizabeth Guttery, daughter of Alexander Guttery and Sarah Guttery his wife, one negro man now in possession of Alexander; also unto Elizabeth Guttery one sorrel mare colt, feather bed and furniture and also my pewter. If said Elizabeth die without lawful issue, then above named legacies to be given to her sister, Sarah Guttery. Ex.: Alexander Guttery. Wit.: William James (X), Hannah Guttery, Joseph Starkey.
Elizabeth Oaks (X)

Page 408: Appraisal of estate of PHINEBAS GLOVER. Taken 21 July 1786, Joseph Taylor, Daniel Boatright, James Thomas. Court 26 July 1786.

Page 409: Will of ORSON MARTIN, dated 24 January 1786, Pro. 24 July 1786. Son, John Martin, all my land on North side of Cat Tail branch, 1 feather bed and furniture when he comes of age; daughter, Jane Martin, feather bed and furniture and 1 bay mare and saddle which she now has; daughter, Mary Martin 1 feather bed and furniture when she comes of age; my wife, Ann Martin, all my land on South side of Cat Tail branch and all the rest of my estate beside what is before mentioned during her widowhood; son, Stephen Martin, one negro boy; daughter, Sarah Martin; son, Orson Martin, land. Exrs.: my two sons, John and Stephen Martin and my wife. Wit.: Jesse Talley, James Boatright, James Bryant.   Orson Martin L.S.

Page 411: Will of ROBERT DOUGLAS, dated 1 April 1785, Pro. 25 September 1786. My wife, Catharine Douglas; son, David, after death of my wife the tract of land I now live on, 295 a.; grandson, Robert Douglas, son of Robert, deceased; 1 part to each of my children: David Douglas, Elizabeth Ransome and Anne Stratton. Exrs.: son, David Douglas and son-in-law, John Stratton. Wit.: Ed. Carrington, Francis Flippen, James Hudgins.

Page 412: Will of WILLIAM PALMER, dated 11 September 1786, Pro. 23 October 1786. Granddaughter, Judith Palmer Carter, land whereon I now live, 175 a. on waters of Deep run. Having already given all my other children not herein named an equal part and their full share of my estate, I do not think it nec-essary to mention them particularly by name as I do not intend giving them any thing more. Exrs.: friend, Robert Furlong and Mayo Carrington, son, Fleming Palmer. Wit.: M. Carrington, Chas. F. Creasy (X), Henry Lynch, Peter Montague.

Page 414: Appraisal of estate of ROBERT DOUGLAS. By: John Flippen, George Walton, Robert Walton. Court 26 September 1786.

Page 416: Will of JOHN STEWART of Littleton Parish, date 25 July 1774, Pro. 27 November 1786. Wife, Catherine; Children: Charles Stewart, Nancy Stewart, James Stewart, John Stewart and Rebeckah Stewart. Exrs.: my wife, Katherine, Nathan Glen and James Glen. Wit.: David Smith, Fannie Smith, Robert Ransome, John Anderson.

Page 417: Inventory and Appraisal of JOHN THOMPSON, date 22 January 1787.

Page 418:   Will of MARY GLOVER, date 25 July 1786, Pro. 26 Feb-
             ruary 1787. Son, Samuel Glover; son, Phinebas Glover;
son, Robert Glover; children of my son Robert Glover. Exrs.:
Nathaniel Carrington, Isaac Bryan. Wit.: John Martin, James
Bryant.   Mary Glover (X)

Page 419:   Account of administration of THOMAS MONTAGUE estate
             with John Montague, administrator. Court 23 July 1787.
Disbursements made to: Thos. Holland, Simon Hughes, Ben Martin,
David Bond, Sarah Walker, James McLaurine, Stephen Cash, John....,
Joseph Clark, Laurence Smith, Thomas Tabb, Wm. C. Hill, Martin
Richardson, Jesse Thomas, Daniel Bates, Jane Montague, William
Turpin, Edmund Logwoods, John Jefferson, John Murry, Isaac Hill,
Charles Scott, John Wiley. Ex. by Ben Wilson and Carry Harrison.

Page 422:   Account of administration of EDMOND PRICE, Mary Price,
             administratrix. To Charles Allen, guardian of James
Anderson (one of items). Court 23 November 1787.

Page 425:   Estate of WM. MC GEHEE. Ex.: Jacob McGehee. By:
             Robert Anderson, Archer Allen, Richd. Booker, John
Ford. Court 29 September 1787.

Page 426:   Will of JAMES WILKIN, date 1 May 1779, Pro. February 25,
             1788. My estate to be sold by my executors; to my
brother, John Wilkins' two daughters, all the money arising from
the sale. Ex.: Archibald Cary and Hickerson Barksdale. Wit.:
William Barksdale, Stith Barksdale.

                              James Wilkins (X)

Page 428:   Will of WILLIAM FRETWELL, dated 29 December 1786, Pro.
             February 25, 1788. Wife, Mary; son, Richard; grand-
son, the heir of my son Richard; grandson, the heir of my son
Joseph Fretwell, deceased; son, Leonard Fretwell; daughter, Nancy
Raine; crop to be sold and money arising to be divided among my
children as hereafter named including 40 pounds in hands of
Leonard Fretwell which he has already received, also 45 pounds in
hands of Thomas Fretwell which he has already received, also 50
pounds in hands of Wm. Byram which he has already received, also
30 pounds in hands of Henry Bohannah which he has already received
these sums as above mentioned being included, I desire the whole
sum to be divided among my children: William, John, Alexander,
James, Thomas, Leonard, Susannah Bohannah, Mary Byram and Nancy
Raine. Ex.: my wife, Mary Fretwell, Wm. and Thomas Fretwell.
Wit.: Thomas Fretwell, Elizabeth Williams (X), James Fretwell,
Reuben Compton and Jos. Michaux.

Page 430:   Inventory and Appraisal of estate of WILLIAM FRETWELL.
             Taken 27 February 1788 by: Anderson Cocke, Saymore
Wright, Stephen Cocke. Court 24th (?) March 1788.

Page 432:   Division of estate of JAMES ANDERSON by Thomas Ander-
             son exor. according to will. Slaves: to Thomas Ander-
son, James Anderson, Peter Francisco and Susanna, his wife, to
Agnes Anderson; 300 acres of land divided among the five daughters of James Anderson according to will; to Mary Raine, 60 a.
adjoining James Anderson, her brother; to Sarah Compton, 60 a.
adjoining the first on the east Roger Williams on the West; to
Elizabeth Legrand, 60 a. South of the last mentioned tract and
adjoining the same parties on the East and West; to Susannah
Francisco, 60 a. South of the last mentioned tract adjoining
Randolph's Sandy Ford tract; to Agnes Anderson, 60 a. West of
Thomas Anderson's tract and divided from the first mentioned

60 a. to Mary Raine by an East and West line adjoining Sandy Ford tract on the South by James Allen....John Woodson....Wm. Lee....

Page 434: Will of OBADIAH HENRDRICK, dated 26 April 1787, Pro. 28 April 1788. Sister-in-law, Elizabeth Hendrick, 100 pounds to the superintendent of the Independent Methodist Church, rest of estate to be divided equally among the following persons to-wit: Obadiah Hendrick, son of Zachariah Hendrick, deceased and Obadiah Hendrick, son of John Hendrick, carpenter and my brother Benjamin Hendrick and Nathaniel Hendrick and Ezekiel Hendrick and Bernard Goode Hendrick son of Bernard Hendrick, deceased and if he should die before he comes of age his part to be equally divided among his own brothers which I give to them. The money arising from the hire of Moses alias Bacchus young Ben Dancy and Almey(?) shall be given to them as soon as collected also the money arising from hire of Martain and Will to be applied to the supporting of old Ben and Bess Harry to be put to some trade at the discretion of my exrs. Exrs.: Philip Ratch , John Finney, Robert Walthal, Job Johnson. Test.: Waddy Thomson, Jesse Davis (X), Fanny Davis (X), Hannah Davis (X), James Philips.

Page 435: Will of JUDITH JONES, dated March 3, 1788, Pro. 23 June 1788. To Judith Bond; to my son, John San-didge; daughter, Mary Thomas; son, Frederick Jones; son, Walter Jones; rest of my estate to be equally divided between my sons, Daniel, James, Frederick Jones and Walter Jones and also the land warrant that is now in Samuel Taylor, Jr. possession except five pounds I gave to Susannah Jones. Ex.: Daniel Jones. Test.: Cornelius Thomas, Abraham Thomas, James Boatright.
Judith Jones (X)

Note: Was not sure if the name was Walter or Waller Jones.

Page 436: Appraisal of estate of SAYMORE SCOTT, ESQ. By: William Evans, Benjamin Hopkins, Roger Williams. Court 23 June 1788.

Page 438: Inventory and appraisal of Estate of JUDITH JONES, deceased. Court 25 August 1788.

Page 438: Will of JOHN BASKERVILLE of Littleton Parish, dated 10 January 1788, Pro. 22 September 1788. Brother Samuel Baskerville, 731 a. whereon I now live on the South side of Willises R. in Cumberland County, also the following slaves...; my brothers and sisters; brothers: George, Richard and William; sisters: Mary Bass and Magdalene Trabue; to brother, George, 100 a. and with....to be laid off according to the discretion of Cary Harrison and Alexander Trent, Jr. Ex.: Brother, Samuel Basker-ville, Cary Harrison. Wit.: John Hill, William Brown, Jno. Miller.
John Baskerville

Page 449: Appraisal of estate of BENJAMIN BOLES (BOWLS),deceased. Jacob Fariss, John Sims, George Woodfin (or Woodson?) Court June 1788.

Will of DRURY WOODSON, dated 7 May 1788, Pro. 24 November 1788. Wife, Lucy; all my children: Judith Johnson, Charles Woodson; daughter, Mary Woodson, daughter, Nancy King, daughter, Elizabeth Woodson, daughter, Martha Woodson; all of which legacies to be paid as they come of age; son, Drury Woodson. Exrs.: my wife, Lucy Woodson and son, Charles Woodson. Wit.: Jesse Talley, Agness Talley, Susanna Foster.
Signed Drury Woodson

Page 443: Appraisal of estate of JOHN BASKERVILLE by Samuel
           Baskerville exor. November 24, 1788 sworn to by:
George Anderson, ...Guttery, Wm. Coleman. Court 27 January 1789.

           Will of WILLIAM CASTILO HILL of Littleton Parish,
           dated 27 February 1788, Pro. 27 January 1789. Wife,
Susanna; my four children: Ann Webb Hill, William Castilo Hill,
Churchwell Hill, Willoughby Suggett Hill; to Isaac Hill and Sarah
Hill, his wife, one negro girl and her increase during their
lives and then to be equally divided between their four children,
Sarah Hill, Thomas Suggett Hill, Castilo Hill and Barber Hill
provided Isaac Hill's estate should all be taken to pay a debt
to Thaddeus Williams and my estate kept clear, the said Isaac
Hill for security for the said Isaac Hill. Ex.: my wife,
Susanna, Isaac Hill, Simon Gentry and Robert Anderson. Wit.:
Dangerfield Harrison, Betty Tapscott, Edney Tapscott, Charles
Allen Merryman, Cynthia H. Merryman.
                              Wm. C. Hill L.S.

Page 445: Appraisal of estate of SAMUEL VAWTER. Thomas Anderson,
           William Anderson, Richard Wilson. Court 23 July 1789.

           Appraisal of estate of ISHAM RICHARDSON. William
           Anderson, Samuel Williams, Benjamin Allen. Court
23 March 1789.

           Appraisal of estate of ANN ROWLAND. By: Jos. Taylor.,
           Richard Taylor, Thomas Taylor. Court October 1788.

Page 449: Inventory of estate of WM. C. HILL taken 3 February
           1789. Court 25 March 1789.

Page 450: Account of Sales of Estate of WILLIAM C. HILL. Buyers:
           Richard Richards, Jesse Merryman, Susannah Hill, Wm.
Powell, George Carrington, Drury Hatcher, Wm. Robeson, Jane Ross-
berry, W. Wilson, Thos. Walton, Wm. Hobson, Wm. Daniel, John
Richardson, James Robeson, Phillip Flippen, Langhorne Tabb,
Beverly Lyott, Thos. Hobson, Thos. Wood, Isham Carter, John
Holman, Anthony Mullins, Wm. Maddox, Ben Wilson, Isaac Hill.
Court March 26, 1789.

Page 453: Appraisal of estate of DRURY WOODSON. Isaack Bryant,
           Jas. Taylor, Thos. Wilkinson. Court 27 April 1789.

Page 454: Report of account of Adm. ABRAHAM SANDIFER. Court
           May 23, 1789. Report of amount due Joanna Sandifer
exor. of will of and Stephen Cocke an exor. By: James Holeman,
Miller Woodson, Anderson Cocke.

Page 455: Further account of estate of JAMES SANDIFER, before
           Tscharner Woodson teste. 20th(?) day....1788.

Page 456: Account of admin. of estate of MICAJAH MOSBY. Account
           began 1772, exhibited by Wm. Smith and approved by:
Richard Crump, V. Markham, John Swann. Court July 27, 1788.

Page 459: Account of admin. of estate of WILLIAM SMITH by Jesse
           Mosby. "We find 15 sh. and 9 pence due Wm. Smith
adm. from Jesse Mossby." Signed: Richard Crump, V. Markham,
John Swann.

Page 459: Court 27 July 1789. This settlement of Wm. Smith adm.
           of Robert Smith with Jesse Mosby was returned and

ordered recorded.

Page 459:   Appraisal of estate of JAMES WILKINS by Gerrollo(?)
            Ellison. 25 February 1788. Court 24 August 1789.

Page 460:   Inventory of estate of SUSANNA JONES orphan of Daniel
            Jones, deceased, given by Nath'l. Carrington, her
guardian.   25 August 1789.

Page 462:   Inventory of estate of FRED'K. JONES, 133 a. land and
            negro boy. Thos. Wilkerson. August 24, 1789.

            Inventory of estate of WALTER (WALLER?) JONES, 133 a.
            land and negro boy by Thomas Wilkerson, guardian.
August 24, 1789.

Page 463:   Will of JOSEPH JOHNS, dated 21 December 1784, Pro.
            26 October 1789. Beloved brother, John Johns, all my
estate. Exors.: beloved brother, John Johns, beloved brother,
Robert Johns. Wit.: Thomas Johns, Sr., Martha Johns (X).
                                        Joseph Johns

Page 464:   Will of MARY WILSON, dated 16 May 1789, Pro. 28 Sept-
            ember 1789. Son, Andrew Wilson; son, Humphrey Wilson.
Test.: Dorothy Hundley, Bartlet Anglea, John Dodson.
                                        Mary Wilson (X)

Page 465:   Will of ISHAM RICHARDSON, dated 15 February 1788. My
            land in Buckingham County, 123 a. on Willises Creek
to be sold and money arisin to pay my debts; my wife, Frances;
three sons Isham, Millenton, and William; three daughters Mary,
Frances and Pattey; my daughter, Ann; daughter, Betty Ann; granddaughter, Sarah Anderson....and if she die without heir, the said
negro boy to revert back to my estate; my daughter, Mary, her son
John (oldest son). Ex.: Benjamin Allen, son of James Allen and
my son, William. Wit.: Samuel Strong, Martha Strong, Agness
Smith (X).   Isham Richardson

At a Court helt at Prince Edward County September (?) 1789 will
of Isham Richardson was presented in court by Frances Richardson,
widow and relict of deceased Isham Richardson. The eldest son
and infant of Isham Richardson came into court and declared that
he was content that the said will be recorded thereupon Patrick
Henry Esq. appointed guardian to Isham Richardson and Millenton
Richardson son of Isham, deceased, infants under age of 21.

Page 467:   Court 26 October 1789. Will of Isham Richardson as
            exhibited by Frances Richardson and it appearing by a
record certified by clerk of district court of Prince Edward
County that the said will as far as related to slaves and personal
estate of decedent be established and it is ordered that same be
recorded and Benjamin Allen and Charles Allen, two of exors.
therein named refusing to act, thereupon option of Frances
Richardson and Miller Woodson who made oath according to law,
letters were granted them with John Holeman and Stephen Cocke
their security.

Page 468:   Inventory and appraisal of MAJOR CHARLES BALLOW. By:
            Marshall Booker, John Griffin, Thomas Hobson. Court
23 November 1789.

Page 469:   Appraisal of estate of ISHAM RICHARDSON. Taken
            August 28, 1789 by: William Anderson, Benjamin Allen,

Charles Allen. Court 23 November 1789.

Page 471: Division of estate of WILLIAM HAMBLETON. James Hambleton, lot; Lucy Hambleton and Susanna Hambleton and the
said James as heirs at law; William V. Hambleton; Jno. M. Hambleton; Ann Hambleton; Elizabeth Hambleton. Pursuant to court order
dated May 1787 estate was appraised by Marshall Booker, John
Griffin and Moses Arnold.

Page 472: Will of GEORGE WRIGHT, dated 4 December 1789, Pro.
26 April 1790. Wife, Mary; my two brothers, William
and Gabriel and brother-in-law, Seymor Wright; my sister-in-law,
Anne Holeman. Exors.: my wife, Mary, William Wright, John Holeman, Jr. Wit.: John Holeman, Stephen Cocke, James Holeman.

Page 473: Will of WARREN WALKER of Littleton Parish, dated
16 Ap(?) 1785, Pro. April 20, 1790. Son, William,
land he now lives on lying on North side of the....branch and
also the negroes and others estate formerly given him and now in
his possession; son, Warren Walker, tract of land whereon he now
lives lying on South side of the broad branch and also negroes
and other estate formerly given him; my wife, Magdalene Walker,
free possession of said land during her natural life; after her
death the land lent her shall be equally divided among my children; daughter, Sarah McGee; daughter, Mary Walker; daughter,
Magdalene Walker; daughter, Judith Walker; my desire is that my
daughters Mary and Magdalene be maintained and educated out of
that part of my estate lent to my wife. Exors.: sons, William
and Warren Walker. Wit.: Wm. B. Rees(?), Stephen Lockett,
Osborn Lockett.   Warren Walker, Sen. L.S.

Page 475: Will of JOHN MINTER of Littleton Parish, dated 3 June
1785, Pro. 27 September 1790. My loving wife (not
named); son, John; daughter, Anne Hannebas. Ex.: son, John
Minter and son-in-law, Henry Hannebas. Wit.: David Winniferd,
Joseph Baughn, Obedience Murphy (X).
                                        John Minter (X)

Written but scratched out: "tho there are several children not
mentioned in this will it can make no odds as there are not being
mentioned with notenable(?) them to any part of testators estate.
                        J. Wilson

Page 476: Inventory of slaves and personal estate of WARREN
WALKER. Taken 10 June 1790, Warren Walker, Magdalene
Walker. Court 28 June 1790.

Page 478: FRANCES CANNIFAX, orphan of James Cannifax, deceased
in account with Wm. Spears, guardian.

        ALICE CANNIFAX, orphan of James Cannifax in account
        with William Spears, guardian. Court 27 September
1790.

Page 478: Estate of WILLIAM FRETWELL in account with James
Fretwell. Paid legatees: William Fretwell, Alex.
Fretwell, James Fretwell, Thomas Fretwell, Leonard Fretwell, Lucy
Bohannon, Jane....Bass(?). Settlement approved by Court 24 Aug-
ust 1790.

Page 480: Will of ABRAHAM CHARLTON of Littleton Parish, dated
1st day of....1790, Pro. 25 October 1790. Wife,
Elizabeth Charlton; son, John, 75 a.; son, Samuel; son, David;

son, James; daughters, Molly Charlton and Sally Charlton; my
children: John, Samuel, David, James, Molly, Sally. Exrs.:
three friends, Hickerson Barksdale, Samuel Williams and William
Russell. Wit.: Wm. Russell, Seamer(?) Lee, Joseph Johns.

Page 482: Will of SAMUEL PHELPS, dated 5 August 1790, Pro.
26 October 1790. Grandson, William James Watkins;
daughter, Peggeth(?) Watkins, 50 a. where she now lives joining
Williams and Henry Perkins line; daughter, Elizabeth Dunkin,
84 a. to be laid off joining Charles Cannons; daughter, Sarah
Coner, land to be laid in Mecklinburgh County joining John
Chamberlaines land and the Lottie(?) lands to be held by her
and her heirs; daughter, Polly Phelps; granddaughter, Masey(?)
Burres; daughter, Patty Phelps; daughter, Nancy Phelps; daughter,
Mary Ann Peck, 5 a. land in Mecklenburg County that her grand-
mother lives on, Mary Chamberlaine. Exrs.: John Phelps of
Charles County and Elizabeth Phelps. Wit.: John Raine, Jr.,
Francis Hurt, Richard Dagnall. Samuel Phelps

Page 484: Will of JOSEPH LEE, dated...., Pro..... Son-in-law,
William Cox; daughter, Keziah Cox; children of my
daughter, Keziah Cox; my wife, Anne Lee, plantation formerly
held by William Lee, 150 a. and 50 a. land to be taken from my
other lands adjoining....150 a. and 50 a. land to be taken from
my other lands....; children of begotten of my daughter, Hezekiah
Cox(?) but should she become a widow, I lend her the said
negroes during her widowhood but at her death or marriage, I
give the negroes unto the children of the said Keziah Cox; unto
my children viz: Anne Lee, Sarah Lee, Joseph Dabb Lee, Mary Lee,
Charles Barnes Lee, William Howell Lee. Ex.: wife, Anne Lee,
Charles Lee, Jr., Matthew Cox. Wit.: William Russell, David
Robertson, Joseph Johns. Signed Joseph Lee L.S.

Page 487: Inventory and appraisal of estate of OBADIAH HENDRICK.
There were many notes on different persons: John
Craddock, Gustavus Hendrick, Bernard Hendrick, John Craddock,
Thomas Octton, Daniel Marshall, John Robertson, John Ramsey and
Charles Lewis, Daniel Justice and Thomas Lester(?), Elizabeth
Hubbard and Oliver West, Samuel Irby and Charles Lewis, Jeremiah
Echols and Jesse Hodges, Leonard Shelton and Benjamin Shelton.
John Baber and Micajah Hampton, Reuben Thornton and John Cotton,
Owen West and John West. Beverley Shelton and Spencer Shelton,
Josiah Echols and Abraham Echols, Richard Priddy and Dudley Glass,
Thomas Priddy and Richard Priddy, John West and Owen West, Daniel
Jenkins, Thomas East and John Brown, Thomas Collins, Edward Lewis
and Charles Lewis, William Williams, Owen West and John West,
Ambrose Morris, Thomas Collins, Anne James, Henry Orendorff,
David Hambrick, Benjamin Hendrick; slaves. Appraised by Daniel
Allen, Benjamin Allen and Alexander Cathry(?). 19 July 1790.

Page 488: Will of RICHARD ALDERSON, dated 2nd March 1783, Pro.
....1791. Son, John, 200 a. land adjoining land of
Thomas Nash and John Hobson; grandson, Booker Alderman, land
adjoining land of Richard Booker and Thomas Nash known by being
called Menanley's; daughter, Rhoda, my plantation whereon I now
live, 50 a.; daughter, Chloe, the remainder part of my land at
the expiration of 16 years containing 100 a.; my negro, Molly,
to my daughter, Chloe, until her daughter arrives to age of 16
and then to her and her heirs forever; slave, Juda, and her
children, namely Polly Branch, Fanny Edmonds, Tarpley Edmonds
and Elisha Edmonds their freedom after my death and the bed and
spinning wheel that she makes use of and the free use of 100 a.
of land for 15 years after my death afterwards to my daughter,

Chloe; I give to my slave Juda, cow and calf, pig, sheep, etc.; daughter, Rhoda, my still; rest of my estate, my three daughters, Betty, Rhoda, Chloe. Exrs.: one name blurred out, Thomas Hobson. Wit.: Wm. Macgehee, Henry Hatcher, Thomas Nash.

Page 492: Inventory of estate of RICHARD ALDERMAN, deceased.
            Taken 6 day January 1791 by: Thomas Nash, Thomas Hobson. Court 26 January 1791.

Page 491: Will of WILLIAM SELF, dated 9 January 1786, Pro.
            24 January 1791. Wife, Hanner Self; son, Thomas Self; rest of my estate to be divided between William Self and ....Kiah ....and Jane(?) Farmer and Jemima Homeby(?) and Matthew Ramsey and Fanny Self, Sary Woolston(?) and Susanna Self and Thomas Self. Exors.: my wife, Hanner Self and William Anderson. Wit.: James Hudgens, Sr., William Bradley, Daniel Coleman.
                                        William Self (X)

Page 492: WIATT ANDREWS of Prince Edward County have empowered
            Robert Smith to sell land in Cumberland County and the money arising thereof to be given to William Andrews (son of Garnett) and William Smith (son of Robert). Ex.: Garnet Andrew, Robert Smith. Wit.: Baker Legrand, John Price, John Slaughter. Date: 4 May 1789, Pro. 24 January 1791 Court.

Page 493: Allotment of dower to SARAH HARRISON, 1180 a. property
            of her late husband, John Langhorne, deceased; to Sary and Cary Harrison, her husband, 390 a. on South side of Willises River beginning at Stephen Woodson Trent's pointers on Horn(?) Quarters road running to George Anderson's land, then to Jeffrey Robertson.... By: Archer Allen, Jeffrey Robertson, Alex. Trent, Jr. Court 25 January 1791.

Page 493-494: Will of THOMAS WRIGHT, dated 12 November 1790,
            Pro. 24 January 1791. Daughter, Mary Thomas; daughter, Elizabeth Glenn; daughter, Susannah Carter; son, Samuel; daughter, Sarah; son, William; daughter, Patsey; son, Josiah; wife, Elizabeth. Ex.: wife, Elizabeth and son, Samuel. Wit.: Thornton Watson, Nathan Womack, Anna Womack.
                                        Signed Thomas Wright

Page 497: Appraisal of estate of SAMUEL PHELPS. November 18,
            1790 by: Wm. Anderson, Jas. Anderson, Thomas Anderson. Court 25 February 1791.

Page 495-497: Appraisal of estate of GEORGE WRIGHT. Sworn to
            by: John Holman, Stephen Cooke, Anderson Cocke, 24 January 1791.

Page 498: Inventory and appraisal of estate of ABRAHAM CHARLTON.
            Sworn to by: Richd. Wilson, David Roberson, Joseph Johns 28 February 1791. Court 28 February 1791.

Page 499: Inventory and appraisal of estate of JOSEPH LEE.
            William Russell, Richard Wilson, Joseph Johns. Court 28 February 1791.

Page 501: Will of SARAH PARKER, dated 16(?) December 1790, Pro.
            28 February 1791. Oldest daughter, Elizabeth Allen Parker (under 18); my two daughters, Elizabeth Parker and Nancy Parker. Ex.: my brother, Jesse Parker and John Holman(?). Wit.: John Hatcher, Simon Gentry.

Page 502: Will of ANN PRICE, dated 17 September 1782, Pro.
            28 February 1791. Granddaughter, Susannah Price, all
my estate. Ex.: Col. Joseph Carrington and Samuel Taylor.
Test.: John Newton, Charles Palmore.

Page 503: Account of admin. of estate of JAMES WILKINS. John
            Woodson, Nath'l. Carrington, Stephen Cocke. Court
28 February 1791.

Page 504: Account of est. JAMES WILKINS by Hickerson Barksdale.

Page 505: Division of estate and allotment of WILLIAM HUDGENS
            estate, February 19, 1791, Samuel Toler and Jane, his
wife, Sally Hudgens, John Hudgens. By: Benjamin Wilson, John
Hatcher. Court 29th March 1791.

Page 507: Account of estate of JOHN LANGHORNE, deceased by
            Sarah Langhorne, exor. Alexander Trent, Jr., Wm.
Powell, Archer Allen. Court 29 March 1791.

Page 509: Inventory and appraisal of MR. MAURICE LANGHORNE at
            Randolph's creek. Taken 5 March 1791, A. Guthrey,
Theo Carter. Court 29 March 1791.

Page....: Account of estate of WILLIAM HUDGINS, deceased by
            James Hudgens, ex. Examined by: Benj. Wilson, John
Hatcher. Court 30 March 1791.

Page 413: Appraisal of estate of DAVID BOWMAN. Richard Taylor,
            John Minter, Joseph Taylor. Court 25 April 1791.

Page 513: Appraisal of estate of SAMUEL GLOVER in obedience to
            court order of 28 February 1791. By: Joseph Taylor,
John Newton, Daniel Jones.

Page 514: Appraisal of estate of THOMAS WRIGHT. By: Charles
            Legrand, John Holman, Jr., Thomas Johns. Court
January 24, 1791. Appr. 27 June 1791.

Page 516: Inventory of estate of ANN PRICE. James Austin, Chas.
            Woodson, Edward Walton. Court 27 .... 1791.

Page 516: Inventory of estate of MARTIN BLAKE. By: John
            Flippen, Simon Gentry, Francis Flippen. Court
January 24, 1792.

Page 517: Inventory of estate of SARAH PARKER, deceased. Taken
            March 1, 1791 by: John Hatcher, Simon Gentry, John
Flippen. Court February 28, 1791.

Page 518: Will of WILLIAM WOMACK, dated 1 January 1786, Pro.
            29 September 1791. Daughter, Judith Hendrick; my son,
Marcenella(?); my seven children: Agnes Sims, William, Charles,
Nathan, Mary, Maxwell and Jesse. Ex.: my four sons, William,
Charles, Nathan and Maxwell (Marcenella?). Test.: Joseph
Starkey, Wm. Richardson, Pehebe Richardson (X).
                                        Wm. Womack

Page 519: Appraisal of estate of WILLIAM CREEDLE, deceased.
            Adm. Ann Creedle. John Murry, Isham Carter, John
Armistead. Court 24 October 1792.

Page 520: Will of JOB THOMAS of Littleton Parish, dated

6 March 1789, Pro. 24 October 1792. Son, Phinebas Thomas, upper half of the land whereon I now live, it being part whereon he now lives; rest to my son, Jesse Thomas. Exr.: Jesse Thomas. Wit.: John Matthews (X), Jesse Hill, William Burton.

Page 521: Appraisal of estate of WILLIAM WOMACK. By: ....Smith, ...Gaines (blurred out), Benj. Allen, Jr., Benj. Allen, Sr. Court 25 April 1792.

Page 523: Appraisal of estate of JOSIAH ROBINSON, deceased. By: John Meador (X), Clement Brown, James Brown. Court 25 April 1792.

Page 524: Will of SIMON GENTRY, dated 8th November 1790, Pro. May 29th 1792. To Betty Thompson, 100 a. land I bought of Jeffrey Robinson provided she gives up right to the land on the road from my house which came by her grandfather, ...McNicoby(?); to Nancy Hatcher and her heirs; to Nancy Hatcher, all my land on North Side of the road whereon the said Nancy now lives, also the negro I bought of John Hatcher, husband to said Nancy; William Thompson, son of Betty; grandson, Thomas Hatcher; my wife (not named); my daughters, Betty and Nancy. Ex.: Neel Thompson and John Hatcher. Wit.: John Jefferson, William Baty.
Signed Simon Gentry

Page 523: Appraisal of estate of SAMUEL TAYLOR, deceased. Thos. Wilkinson, Daniel Boatright, Jos. Boatright. Court 23 July 1792.

Page 526: Appraisal of estate of JOHN SMITH. By: William Davenport, Alex. Banks, Walter Keeble. Court 23 July 1792.

Compiled by
Ella E. Lee Sheffield

FLEMING (cont.) Susanna
26; Tarlton 11; Thomas
11,26,40; William 11,
26,28,40,53,55
FLIPPEN, Ann 9,13; Anne 9,
10; Elizabeth 9,13,44;
Francis 44,63,67,72,77,
82,90; Henry 26; Jacob
44,79; Jane 44; Jno. 71;
John 16,44,60,63,72,73,
79,82,90; Joseph 75;
Martha 44,79; Mary 44,
75,79; Philip 44,85;
Ralph 9,10,13,16,23,40,
43,44,46,79; Robert 13,
16,44,71; Sarah 13;
Thos. 9,10,13,80; Wm.
9,16,44,45
FLIPPING, Frances 59
FLOURNOY, Elizabeth 4,7,
19; Samuel 4,15,17,19,
20,25,26,27,28,30,41,42,
62; Ursley 4; William
25
FOLKS, John 81
FORD, Daniel 7; James 7;
John 4,7,79,81,83;
Judith 7; Mary 7; Peter
7; Sandy 83,84
FORE, Daniel 8; Judith 4
FORGERSON, William 80
FORMBY, Nicholas 26
FORSEE, Ann 53; Charles
26,53; Elizabeth 53;
Francis 26,53; Jane 53;
Joan 30; John 17,26,28,
53; Judith 53; Mary
Ann 26,53; Stephen 17,
26,30,44,53; William
26,53
FOSTER, George 59; James
71,75; Martha 59; Mary
59; Nancy 70; Sarah 70,
71; Susanna 59,84
FRANKLIN, John 9; Joseph
26,28
FRANCISO, Peter 83; Sus-
anna 83
FRAYSER, William 70
FRAZER, Jernimah 7
FRENCH, Hugh 55
FRETWELL, Alexander 83,87;
James 83,87; John 83;
Joseph 83; Leonard 83,
87; Mary 83; Nancy 83;
Richard 83; Susannah
83; Thomas 83,87; Tho-
mas Freeman 1,20;
William 83,87
FUQUA, Elizabeth 60; John
60; Mary 7; William 7
FUQUAY, Joseph 5; William,
Junr. 5
FURLONG, John 74; Richard
11; Robert 82
GAINES, _____ 91; Bernard
65
GANNAWAY, John 7
GARRETT, James 67; William
67
GENINGS, Mary 66
GENKINS, Elizabeth 25
GENTRY, Simon 23,24,41,44,
45,46,49,59,63,69,70,
71,77,79,85,89,90,91
GIBSON, Elizabeth 13,14;
John, Sr. 13; Thomas 13
GILES, _____ 29; Perrin 4
GILLENTINE, Rachel 23
GILLIAM, Charles Manning
57; James 57,59,81;
Jas., Jr. 53; John 30;
Robert 57; Sally 57

GILLS, John 6
GINKINS, Joseph 31
GIPSON, John 58; John, Sr.
13; Mary 58
GLASS, Dudley 88
GLEN, James Coleman 59;
Lucy 43,47; Nathan 21,
39,45,47,82; Nathaniel
43; Nehemiah 43,45,66
GLENN, Ann 43,47,49; Dru-
cilla 59,61; Elizabeth
89; Frances 62; Gideon
21,59,61; James 45,82;
James, Sr. 66
GLOVER, Elizabeth 80;
John 80; Lucy 80; Mary
80,83; Phenibas 12,45,
80,81,82,83; Robert 80,
83; Samuel 80,83,90
GODSEY, John 4; Thomas 4
GOLDIE, Robt. 3
GODD, Alice 47; Elizabeth
4; Lucy 47; Mary 18,
47; Robert 4; Sally 47;
Thomas 47; William 47
GOODE, Bennett 4,7,17,23,
47,55,59,60; John 47;
Mack 28; Martha 18,47;
Nich. 69; Sarah 13
GOODWIN, Ann 4; Isaac 4
GOOG, Mary 4
GORDAN, Robert 66
GORRE, Daniel 2
GOSS, Mary Ann 5
GRAVES, Wm. 28
GRAY, William 58
GREEN, Hugh 53; John 65;
Thomas 75
GRIBBS, John 13
GRIFFIN, John 86,87; Mary
60
GRONG, Lewis 67
GUERRANT, Daniel 2,3,48,
61; David 2; Esther 2;
Jane 2; John 2; Judith
2; Magdalene 2,3; Mary
49,61; Peter 1,2,3
GUILLIAM, James 68
GUNTER, Sarah 13
GUTHREY, _____ 60; A. 90;
Alex 62,73; Eleanor 61;
Thomas 44,62; William
61
GUTTERY, _____ 85; Alex.
53; Alexander 82, Ber-
nard 49; Eleanor 61;
Elizabeth 82; Grissell
49; Hannah 82; Henry
49; Mary 61; Orania 49;
Patty 49; Peter 61;
Philadelphia 49; Sarah
47,49,82; Susanna 49;
William 61; William
Coleman 49
GWYN, Sally 76
HAIRFIELD, David 18
HALL, John 4,78; Philip
78; Thos. 1,11,20,21,
25,29,49
HALLES, Thomas 2
HAMBLETON, Ann 49,67,68,
70,87; Elizabeth 87;
Elley 68; James 67,87;
Jno. M. 87; John Mosby
68; Lucy 68,87; Martha
25; Mary Sims 68; Polly
70; Susanna 68,87; Will-
iam 25,49,50,67,68,69,
77,87; William Terry
67,68; William V. 87
HAMBRICK, David 88
HAMLEY, Thos. T. 10
HAMMAN, Agnes 16; Douty

HAMMAN (cont.) 16; John
16; John, Sr. 16;
Joseph 16
HAMMONTREE, Harris 81;
William 73
HAMPTON, Micajah 88
HANCOCK, Ann 22; George 29,
38,40; James 12; John
22,23,41; Martha 22,41;
Matthew 22; Samuel 22,
41; William 22
HANDCOCK, Nancy Allen 71
HANDRAKE, Zachariah 63
HANES, Peter 47; Samuel 64
HANKLA, James 41
HANNAWAY, John, Jr. 7
HANNEBAS, Anne 87; Henry 87
HARLAND, Vincent 58
HARMAN, Danderfield 79;
Edward 79; Henry 79;
Tabitha 79
HARRIS, Ann 7,16,61,77;
Benj. 2,3,4,7,8,16,18,
19,23,27,53,64,66; Ead-
ith 7; Edith 64; Eleanor
61; Elizabeth 61; Fran-
ces 40; Francis 27;
Henry 61; James 2,4,7,
8,12,27,42,55; John 3,
4,7,21,27,61,64; John,
Sr. 7; Joseph 14,53,54;
Mary 7,27,42,61,64,77;
Nancy 64; Pamela 77;
Peter 53,61,62; Pheba
27,64; Priscilla 64;
Richard 56,62; Sarah 4,
7,8,27,60,64; Simeon 55;
Susannah 61; Tabitha 19;
Thomas 27; William 4,7,
8,13,15,27,41,42,56,79;
William Wagner 64
HARRISON, C. H. 62; Cary
65,81,83,84,89; Danger-
field 85; Elizabeth 7;
John 8; Molley 8; Sam-
uel 8; Sarah 7,89; Will-
iam 7,8,9
HARVEY, Thomas 74
HASKINS, _____ 29; Creed
23,38,68,70,71,73,79;
Edward 42; Robt. 39,58;
Thomas 30,43
HATCHER, Archibald 65,73;
Ben 29; Benj. 59; Ben-
jamin 59,76,80; Betty
76,91; Chas. 29; Drury
81,85; Elizabeth 68;
Frederick 20,31,42,44,
46,57,58,64,65,66,68,
70,71,72,76,77,80;
Henry 4,13,65,89; John
76,89,90,91; Josiah 13,
60,76; Mary 59,76; Nancy
91; Nicholas 66; Sarah
26,76; Susahha 59,76;
Thomas 91
HAY, John 16
HAZLEWOOD, Elizabeth 74
HENDRICK, Adolphus 23;
Allice 23; Benjamin 23,
68,84,88; Bernard 84,
88; Bernard Goode 84;
Betty 23; Christiana
23; Elijah 76; Eliza-
beth 76,84; Ezekiel 84;
Gustavus 88; James 76;
Jane 23; John 23,76,84;
Judith 90; Martha 76;
Mary 23; Moses 23;
Nathaniel 84; Obediah
76,84,88; Rachel 23;
Rebeckah 76; William
23,76; Zachariah 49,51,

HENDRICK (cont.) 84; Zack-
ary 50,76
HENNINGTON, _____ 18
HENRY, Patrick 86
HICKS, Clayborne 62; Eliza-
beth 62; Henry 62; Jesse
62; John 62; Joseph 43;
Mary 62; Nathaniel 62;
Susanna 62
HILL, Ann 53; Ann Webb 85;
Barber 85; Barchenay
53; Betsy 73; Betty 73;
Caley 73; Castilo 85;
Dennett 53; E. 73;
Edward 64; Elizabeth 51;
Frances 73; Hannah 51;
Isaac 73,83,85; James
53; Jesse 73,91; John
51,53,73,84; Joseph 51,
53,72; Joyce 51; Mary
53; Sarah 53,73,85;
Silvanis 16; Sugt. 68;
Susanna 85; Thomas 51,
53,72,73,77; Thomas
Hobson 73; Thomas Sug-
gett 67,68,69,70,73,75,
85; Thos. J. 66,73;
William 49,51,53,72,75;
William Castilo 43,85;
Willoughby Suggett 85;
Wm. 21,66,68; Wm. C.
69,73,75,83,85
HIX, John 14; William 34,
68
HOBSON, Adcock 20,29,31,
41,46,54,55,58,63,64,
67,68; Caleb 68; Dru-
cilla 65; Edward 67;
Eliza 68; Elizabeth 23,
68; Frances 23,66; Fred-
erick 55; Henry 10;
Jacob 68; James 25; Jo-
anna 42,68; John 19,20,
23,30,65,81,88; Lawson
68; Lucy 67,68; Mary
23; Nancy 65; Samuel 24,
27,46,48; Sarah 65,66;
Susanna 65; Thomas 65,
68,77,80,85,86,89; Will-
iam 10,11,19,23,24,31,
42,63,65,68,76,81,85;
Winniferd 68
HODGE, Thos. 2
HODGES, Christian 1; Drury
1; Edm'd. 1; Jesse 88;
Johnson 49; Mary 1;
Thomas 1; William 1
HODNETT, Mary 45
HOGAN, Daniel 33,34,35,36,
37; Elizabeth 29
HOLAND, Charles 14; John
66; Thomas 68
HOLEMAN, James 7,85; John
41,47,55,86
HOLLAND, Ann 39; Anne 41;
Charles 28,54; Charlotte
39; Francis 77; James
22,23,39,41,70,76,77;
Jane 16,41; Jean 22;
John 22,39,40,41,66;
Jonas Meader 76,77;
Margaret 39,70; Martha
75,77; Mary 69; Samuel
22; Sarah 77; Spearman
39; Thomas 22,40,41,71,
83; William 16,20,23,
39,41,44,68; William,
Jr. 22,41
HOLLOWAY, Billey 77; Cath-
ron 39; Drucilla 14,34,
35,36,37,38; Frances 69;
Hannah 14,38,68,69;
Hannah Spiers 69; James
14,22,23,28,30

HOLLOWAY (cont.) 14,22,23,
28,30,68,77; Jane 14;
John 4,10,14,33,34,36,
37,38; Martha 14; Phebe
14,34,35,36,37,38,39;
Sam 68; Samuel 14,28,
41,69,73,77; Sarah 14,
34,35,36,37,38,39;
William 14,37
HOLMAN, Ann 87; Henry 19,
64; James 8,10,12,19,
21,87; James, Jr. 13;
Jane 19; Jno. 77; John
19,61,65,66,69,72,77,
78,79,85,87,89,90;
John, Jr. 87; Mary 19,
87; Sarah 19; Susanna
77; William 19
HOLMES, James 21
HOLT, Betty 26; John 26,
27,42,71,78; Tabitha 26
HOMEBY, Jemima 89
HOMESLY, Ann 35; Benjamin
64
HOOD, Joseph 66
HOOPER, Elizabeth 4,61;
George 4,61; Hugh 4;
Joseph 4
HOPKINS, Benjamin 84;
Edward 69; Francis 20;
Jane 20
HOPPER, Booth 3
HOPSON, Henry 18,20; Wm.
13
HORTON, John 22
HOSKINS, Edward 27
HOWARD, _____ 15; Anne 18;
Benjamin 18; Cary 18;
Elizabeth 18; Lockey
18; Martha 18; Mary 18,
49; Rebbecca 18; Will-
iam 4,11,27
HOWELL, William 31
HOWLETT, Betty 46
HOYLE, Mary 4; Nicholas 4;
Nicholas, Jr. 4
HUBBARD, Allice 23; Ann
39; Anna 73; Elizabeth
88; John 15,31; Joseph
33,34,35,40,67,77,81;
Moses 69,75,81; Nancy
73
HUCKABEY, John 41
HUDGENS, Drury 68; Hollo-
way 68; James 34,35,36,
41,44,70,71,80,82,89,
90; Jean 71; Jno. 36;
John 36,37,71,90; Lu-
zey 44; Martha 14; Mary
14,36,37; Moses 44,51;
Polly 71; Robert 36,37,
41,68; Sally 71,90;
William 36,37,63,64,67,
71,72,90
HUDSON, Robert 4
HUGGINS, James 22
HUGHES, Abraham 18; Anderson 80; Ann 18,19; An-
thony2,30; Archelaus
60; Ashford 1,9; Caleb
30,68; David 18; Eliza-
beth 2,6,10,18,30; Em-
erich 49; Francis 18;
Isaac 8,13,14,17; Jane
10; Jesse 18; John 6,
10,11,18,20,26,34,46,
47,53,55,59,60; John,
Jr. 10; Joseph 6,9,10,
41; Josiah 30,31; Jud-
ith 6,55; Leander 41;
60,63; Martha 9,12,13,
17,18,34,44; Mary 8;
Micajah 31; Orlando 30,

40,41; Povall 60; Powell
60; Robert 6,9,12,18,19,
21,34; Sarah 9; Simon
26,29,44,51,60,67,72,
75,83; Stephen 1,3,6,7,
60; Susanna 9; Temper-
ance 9; Thomas 18,68;
William 16,23,29,51,68,
74
HUNDLEY, Dorothy 71,86
HUNTER, Col. _____ 26
HURT, Francis 88
INGRAHAM, Glasgow 46
IRBY, Samuel 88
IRVINE, James 73; John 73
ISOM, James 81
JAME, Sam 2
JAMES, Anne 88; Elizabeth
17,31,34,35; Francis 3,
7,9,17,31; Francis, Jr.
5,31; John 5; Mary 7,17,
18; Richard 26,29,34,35,
68,81; William 82
JEFFERSON, Elizabeth 49,57;
Jno. 53,66,67; John 43,
48,49,52,72,83,91; Thom-
as 24
JENKINS, Daniel 88; John
34,35; Joseph 31,33,34,
35,40,50,59,68,70,71;
Lucy 59,71
JENNING, Mary 8
JINKIN, Joseph 31
JOBSON, Philip Yates 51
JOHNS, Jane 55,60; Jesse
72,81; John 55,60,72,86;
Joseph 9,50,60,86,88,89;
Judy 60; Martha 72,86;
Marthy 60; Robert 5,22,
55,60,72,86; Thomas 5,
81,86,90; William 55,60
JOHNSON, Anne 13; Collins
26; Daniel 1,27,28,64;
Elizabeth 1,41; James
28; Jas. 27; Jeremiah
28; Job 41,42,44,63,68,
84; John 1,9,13,18,28,
34,35,36,37,62; Joseph
9,18,34,35,36,37,62;
Martha 9,34,35,36,37;
Mary 1,28,41,42,44;
Nathaniel 27; Phene 1,
28; Randolph 41,42,44;
Rebecca 42; Samuel 77;
Sarah 9,28; Thomas 13,
42; William 13,36
JONES, Ann 62; Beetsee 73;
Daniel 73,75,81,84,86,
90; Frederick 73,84,86;
Guinivere 62; Harrison
78,80; James 84; John
26,50,62,67,80,84;
Judith 73,84; Mary 18,
62,73,84; Mary Ann 80;
Michael 31; Sale 73;
Sam'l. 20,23,62; Sarah
18,80; Susanna 62,73,84,
86; Waller 73,84,86;
Walter 73,84,86; William
62,63
JONS, Jane 60; John 60;
Joseph 60; Judy 60;
Marthy 60; Robert 60;
William 60
JUSTICE, Daniel 88
KEEBLE, Dorothy 76; Hum-
phrey 76,77; Walter 76,
91
KEELING, G. 78; George 81
KEEN, Carroll 49
KEON, Carrell 14
KERR, William 64
KEVIL, Thomas 68

WILLIAMS (cont.) 83,84;
Samuel 57,69,70,73,74,
75,78,85,88; Sarah 65,
69; Susanne 69; Thad-
deus 69,74,75; Thomas
69,74,75; William 18,
51,69,88
WILLIAMSON, George 10,11;
Robert 10,38
WILMORE, Daniel 55
WILSON, Andrew 86; Ben 40,
53,83,85; Benjamin 22,
41,50,62,67,77,90;
Elizabeth 62; Humphrey
86; Mary 86; Richard
85,89; W. 81,85
WINFREE, Ann 49; Charles
49; Isaac 41,49,71;
Israel 8,21,29; Jacob
9,41,49,71; Jacob, Jr.
22,41; Jane 49; John
4; Sarah 49,75; Valen-
tine 28,29
WINFREY, Henry 4; Jacob
74; John 9
WINNFORD, Charles 62,69;
David 61,62,63,87;
George 13,61,69; Wil-
moth 31,69
WITT, Benjamin 20; Mary 20
WOMACK, Agnes 90; Anna 89;
Charles 90; Jesse 90;
Judith 90; Marcenella
90; Mary 90; Maxwell
90; Nathan 73,76,77,81,
89,90; William 15,90,91
WOOD, Sally 62; Stephen
6; Thos. 85; William 65
WOODFIN, George 80,81,84
WOODSON, _____ 17,56,57;
Benjamin 14,15; Charity
10; Charles 45,63,79,
84,90; Charles, Jr. 26;
Drury 59,70,71,75,79,
84,85; Elizabeth 1,6,
28,84; George 72,73,84;
Hughes 10; Jane 10;
Jesse 10,75,79; Jessey
70; John 1,5,11,15,21,
52,55,56,61,65,69,73,
74,77,78,79,81,84,90;
John, Jr. 47,48,63;
John James 66; John P.
81; John Pleasants 80;
Jos. 20; Joseph 9,12,
15,21,69,82; Josiah 70,
71; Judith 84; Lamburn
10; Lucy 57,69,84; Mar-
tha 84; Mary 9,17,40,
54,79,84; Mary Ann 10;
Mathew 49; Miller 61,
69,70,77,78,79,85,86;
Nancy 84; Obediah 7;
Sanborn 12; Sarah 9,54;
Shadrack 79; Stephen
51,57; Tscharner 85;
Tucker 2,15,34,40,46,
54,80,81; Wade 54;
William 79
WOOLDRIDGE, Dan 36,37,40;
Daniel 37,38; David 20;
Edward 65; Elizabeth
20; Frances 20; Henry
20,37,38,40; Jno. 40;
John 20,37,38,49; Jo-
seph 20,36,37,38; Mar-
tha 20; Mary 20,36,37;
Robert 4,65; Thos. 20,
21,36,38
WOOLDRIGE, Thos. 2
WOOLSTON, Sary 89
WORLEY, Christian 14;
Elizabeth 14; Esther 13;

WORLEY (cont.) John 13;
Jude 14; Mary 13; Will-
iam 13
WORSHAM, Thomas 40
WRIGHT, Archibald 57,79;
Elizabeth 45,89; Gab-
riel 57,79,87; George
2,57,61,69,72,78,79,
87,89; Griffin 57,66;
Henry 57,79; John 48,
69; Josiah 89; Mary
57,79,87,89; Rachel 71;
Sally 79; Samuel 52,89;
Sarah 57,79,89; Saymore
83; Seymore 87; Susan-
nah 89; Thomas 45,47,
57,66,70,73,79,89,90;
William 57,79,87,89
YARBROUGH, Edward 12;
Elizabeth 12; Hannah 12
YOUNG, John 4
_____, Anthony 30; Benj.
12; Carenlius 11; Dan-
iel 57; Edward 4; Fred-
erick 68; John 27,53,
78,83; Lottie 88; Rich-
ard 2; William 12,22